Rethinking
ASIA

Why Asia is Hopeful

Rethinking Asia 4
Why Asia is Hopeful

May 3, 2018
Copyright © 2018 by Center for Asia Leadership Initiatives
Printed in Kuala Lumpur, Malaysia
A Publication of the Center for Asia Leadership Initiatives
Acumen Publishing
14 Nancy Lane Waltham MA 02452 USA

Center for Asia Leadership Initiatives
Website: www.asialeadership.org
Facebook: www.facebook.com/asiagroup

Asia Leadership Trek
Website: www.asialeadershiptrek.org
Facebook: www.facebook.com/asialeadershiptrek
Twitter & Weibo: @Asia_Trek

All rights reserved. No part of this book may be reprinted or reproduced or utilized in any form or by any electronic, mechanical, or other means, now known or hereafter invented, including photocopying and recording, or in any information storage or retrieval system, without permission in writing from the publisher.

Library of Congress Control Number 2018941353
KDP ISBN: 979-8-3382662-4-3
US $13.99

For inquiries on partnership or sponsorship, or purchase of the publication, please email us at: cali@asialeadership.org

Disclaimer: This book is designed to provide information and motivation to our readers. It is sold with the understanding that the publisher is not engaged to render any type of psychological, legal, or any other kind of professional advice. The content of each article is the sole expression and opinion of its author, and not necessarily that of the publisher. No warranties or guarantees are expressed or implied by the publisher's choice to include any of the content in this volume. Neither the publisher nor the individual author(s) shall be liable for any physical, psychological, emotional, financial, or commercial damages, including, but not limited to, special, incidental, consequential or other damages. Our views and rights are the same: You are responsible for your own choices, actions, and results.

Why Asia is Hopeful

9 inspiring essays written by scholars from Harvard, Tufts, and MIT who traveled through 14 cities in 11 countries in 2017

RETHINKING ASIA

4

Edited by Hungsoo S. Kim

ACUMEN™
PUBLISHING

To all the aspiring leaders of this world

| Table of Contents |

•••

About the Editor   9
About the Contributors   11
Foreword   15

Introduction

| Introduction | Leading the Growth of Leadership Education in Asia

Hungsoo S. Kim 21

Part 1 • Fellowship Essays

| Chapter 1 | Reflections on Design Thinking in Asia

Helen van Baal 35

| Chapter 2 | Topia: Educating Young Leaders on Adaptive Leadership in Dynamic Asia

Ami Valdemoro 59

| Chapter 3 | Teaching Adaptive Leadership in Kyrgyzstan: Work in Practice and Reflections

Philipp Essl, Umar Shavurov and Hungsoo S. Kim 77

Part 2 • Asia Leadership Trek Essays

| Chapter 4 | Onwards with Zeal and Zest: An Engineer's Perspective on Continuous Leadership Learning

Puay Siang Tan 99

| Chapter 5 | Disrupt Yourself and Your Business Before You Get Disrupted

Jennifer Hurford 125

| Chapter 6 | A Comparison: Policies, Society, and Culture in Asia and Peru

Giacomo Declercq 149

| Chapter 7 | Does the Global News Media Get Asia Right?

Raza Ahmad 165

| Chapter 8 | Vietnam: Growth of the Lotus Nation

Ralph Poettinger 185

| Chapter 9 | What Great Leaders Do Differently, Part 2

Hungsoo S. Kim 207

Editor's Acknowledgments	220
Appendix I: Trek and Fellowship Itinerary	226
Appendix II: List of Trekkers and Fellows	239

| About the Editor |

•••

Hungsoo S. Kim, a Korean national, is the Co-founder and President of the Center for Asia Leadership Initiatives. Passionate about nurturing and empowering talents in Asia, he has been actively engaging various stakeholders in developing and running over twenty-five programs in more than twenty-two countries in Asia to help emerging leaders explore opportunities to be socially responsible in facing the region's complex challenges. These programs fall under the Center's four main initiatives, namely the Asia Leadership Trek, a public diplomacy arm for scholars at Harvard, Stanford, MIT, and Fletcher; the Asia Leadership Institute, a leadership capacity-building arm; the Acumen Case Center, a research and content development arm; and Acumen Publishing, a publication arm. Hungsoo oversees these initiatives, along with a team of twenty comprising Faculty and Teaching Fellows from Harvard and Stanford University, and administrators at the main office in Boston, U.S., and the Asian regional headquarters in Kuala Lumpur, Malaysia.

As part of his continuous endeavor toward grooming leaders of tomorrow, Hungsoo recently joined the Asia Future Institute, a Seoul-based policy and leadership think tank, as Executive Director to instill in Korean and Northeast Asian talents the drive and passion to create positive social change through effective leadership. He prides himself on accelerating efforts to reach out to all forty-eight countries in Asia by 2022. Hungsoo's areas of research and training, among others, include 'Negotiation and Mediation,' 'Adaptive Leadership,' 'Persuasion and Influence,' and 'Creative Confidence.' To date, some twenty-five thousand burgeoning and established leaders from the government, non-profits, and corporate world in Asia have benefited from these programs.

Prior to establishing the Center, Hungsoo worked for twelve years in varying sectors from strategy consulting and social entrepreneurship to international development, politics, and government. He has also served as a policy aide in the United Nations in New York representing Korea, and as a project analyst at UNESCO in Paris. He currently sits on the board of two non-profit organizations, and has served as a visiting scholar at the Asia Center at Harvard University and at the Kellogg School of Management in Northwestern University. Hungsoo holds a Masters of Public Administration from the Harvard Kennedy School of Government; Masters in International Cooperation from the Graduate School of International Studies, Seoul National University; and completed his undergraduate studies with two majors in U.S. and International Law, and International Politics with a minor in Economics from Handong University.

Previously, Hungsoo was the editor of seven books, namely *Rethinking Asia Vol. 1: Education and Innovation, Rethinking Asia Vol. 2: Entrepreneurship and Economic Development, Rethinking Asia Vol. 3: Social and Political Change, Finding the Leaders in Us: New Goals for the Future, Redefining Success: Learning to Lead for Change, Next Generation Leadership: Empower Youth to Shape the Future of Asia,* and *Leaders in Development: Enhancing Your Leadership Effectiveness in a Changing World.*

| About the Contributors |

•••

Hungsoo S. Kim is the Co-founder and President of the Center for Asia Leadership Initiatives. Passionate about nurturing and empowering talents in Asia, he has developed and organized over twenty-five programs in more than twenty-two countries in the region to help budding leaders enhance their leadership competencies to navigate challenges in the 21st century. Hungsoo aims to engage with youth in all forty-eight countries in Asia by 2022 and inspire them to enact change in the world.

Helen van Baal is a strategic designer, teacher and design thinking expert with a focus on projects within the social innovation and education realm. Helen has taught design in many countries across Europe, South America, Africa and Asia. Between 2013 and 2015 she was a program lead at the HPI School of Design Thinking in Germany where she designed, managed and co-led the academic education in Design Thinking as well as supported student teams in developing innovative ideas and founding successful start-ups. Apart from her work with students, Helen has worked as a designer and innovation consultant with large corporations, non-profits, start-ups and consultancies within various industries (i.e. banking, education, automotive, digital and product design), teaching, consulting and designing globally (Europe, Americas, Africa, Asia, Australia). At the core of her work is the belief in empathy as the basis for good design and the dedication to creating value through design.

Ami Valdemoro is a leadership coach, social change agent, health advocate, and entrepreneur. She is the Founder and Chief Empowerment Officer of Three Points Ventures, Inc., a firm specializing in strategy, execution, and leadership development for nonprofits and businesses working in the social impact sector. Ami's experience spans five continents, beginning with a tenure at the African Tobacco Control Consortium, a five-year Bill and Melinda Gates Foundation-funded program for the American Cancer Society's global tobacco control unit. From March 2016 to March 2017, she was the Executive Director of Friends of Hope, a social business dedicated to creating access to opportunities for Filipinos to prosper. Prior to that, she was the Executive Director of Hands On Manila, a non-profit organization focused on providing volunteer service opportunities to organizations and groups in Metro Manila. She currently sits on the board of MyShelter Foundation and Liter of Light USA, two social enterprises dedicated to empowering lives around the world through community-built solar lighting technologies. Ami graduated with honors from Georgetown University's Edmund A. Walsh School of Foreign Service in 2006, and earned her Masters in Public Policy from the Harvard Kennedy School in 2013. In 2017, Ami served as a Teaching Fellow in the Practice of Adaptive Leadership at the Center for Asian Leadership, training thousands of young students and mid-career professionals on how to be effective change agents in their organizations and communities.

Philipp Essl has worked extensively on the implementation of corporate sustainability practices and broader private sector development to drive positive socio-economic change across more than twenty countries in South East Asia, Latin America, and (North & West) Africa. He has also taught numerous students and professionals in the practice of adaptive leadership and interest-based negotiation. Philipp holds an MBA from the Vienna University of Economics and Business Administration and a MPA from the Harvard Kennedy School, where he continues to coach students in the practice of adaptive leadership.

Umar Shavurov holds a MPA from the Harvard Kennedy School and MA in International Relations and Conflict Resolution from the University of Salvador (Argentina). He also holds a Diploma in International Relations from the Kyrgyz State University. He worked extensively over the last decade internationally on public sector reforms in Latin America, West Africa, and Central Asia. During 2017 fall term Umar taught an inaugural course on adaptive leadership at the American University in Central Asia.

Puay Siang Tan is currently pursuing her second Masters at MIT's System Design and Management (SDM) Program which is a hybrid program that deepens one's technical competency in the engineering field and sharpens management skills with leadership training from Sloan School of Management. She is also part of a research group at MIT – Global Teamwork Lab focusing on team dynamics and team learning. In applying systems thinking approach, her thesis work involves studying into how teams across various functional groups interact and if the behavior of the teams affect the project outcomes. Puay Siang is passionate about promoting science and engineering to the younger generation and has presented as a speaker in a nation-wide symposium to encourage more female students to join the engineering discipline. She feels her training in Mechanical Engineering has provided her translational skillsets to open up multiple pathways in her professional pursuit in biomaterials engineering, defense engineering and systems thinking and systems engineering. Puay Siang is also active in her social community in initiating and organizing community bonding events to help foster social cohesiveness and inclusivity.

Jennifer Hurford is a Director at the Integrated Strategy Team at VML, a global digital marketing agency helping clients innovate their communications and marketing processes. She is passionate about reinventing how companies connect with consumers and interested in combining business strategy and human-centered design principles to help organizations create delightful customer experiences and exceed financial targets. A universal truth is that we have a fundamental human need to connect with one another and at VML, Jennifer loves to help brands fulfill that need and make them truly matter to people. Jennifer has a depth of knowledge in leveraging customer insights and market trends to produce meaningful consumer experiences within the digital ecosystem. Her work includes rebranding and transformation of digital strategy for CPG, retail, financial institutions, real estate, late stage VC-backed start-ups as well as non-profits. She is one of five MBA graduates selected globally for WPP's 2017 MBA Fellowship program. The WPP MBA Fellowship is an executive program created to develop high-caliber management talent with experience across a range of disciplines. While completing three one-year rotations, fellows are placed in senior roles at WPP's leading global companies, and work with some of the world's most valued brands. With a background in business strategy at IDEO, an innovation and design consulting firm, Jennifer brings a fluency in design thinking tools required to inspire transformation within global brands. Prior to IDEO, she worked at Citigroup's Corporate Bank covering Consumer Brands and Healthcare clients in London, New York, Frankfurt and Cairo. She received graduate degrees from Harvard Business School and the Kennedy School of Government. She also holds a BA in Economics from Haverford College.

Giacomo G. Canepa is the Co-founder of Capital Tech Latam a Financial Consulting Company based in Miami, Florida, especially dedicated to attend Latin America. Prior to establishing Capital Tech Latam, he worked in the financial services sector from the public side in the Peruvian Central Bank, from the multilateral side in the World Bank and the International Forum of Sovereign Wealth Funds and from the private sector as an investment banker. He holds a Master in International Business from The Fletcher School and a BSC in Economics from ESAN University.

Raza Ahmad is an M.A. Candidate at the Fletcher School of Law and Diplomacy at Tufts University. Raza's focus at Tufts is on International Communication and Leadership in Global Corporations. As the child of immigrants from Asia, Raza is deeply committed to furthering his understanding of the region, as well as increasing links between Asia and the United States. He previously completed his B.A. in Political Science from the University of California, Davis. While not pursing his degree,

Raza is usually playing soccer, producing videos, or traveling around the world.

Ralph Poettinger is a managing director at Alpine Group with about € 100 million in assets under management. He also acts as a globally active advisor, author, and speaker on value-driving corporate development for strategically growing his clients' enterprises, and is a lecturer on corporate finance at the Vienna University of Economics and Business. Ralph graduated in July 2016 from the Master of Laws in International Business Law (LL.M.) programme of the National University of Singapore, conducted in Singapore as well as Shanghai, China, in cooperation with the East China University of Political Science and Law. His formative years have inspired him to pursue an international career in the fields of financial and professional services in nine countries. In the past, Ralph has gathered experience at the Liechtenstein office of Hong-Kong-owned Bendura Bank, and at the London office of Chicago-based investment bank William Blair & Company, as well as in one of Austria's leading boutique M&A law firms. Outside of work, he is involved with a host of not-for-profit organizations, for which Ralph has held a variety of positions with an emphasis on educative programs for the younger generations.

| Foreword |

•••

    The people's representatives will reach their destination, invested with the highest confidence and unlimited power. They will show great character. They must consider that great responsibility follows inseparably from great power. To their energy, to their courage, and above all to their prudence, they shall owe their success and their glory.

    The tremendous economic and political growth shown by Asia over the last few decades reminds me of the the above passage, taken from a collection of decrees made by the French National Convention on May 8, 1793. As a lecturer in public policy at the Harvard Kennedy School and an advisor for political campaigns and candidates, I feel strongly that great responsibility must follow the great impact that Asia is currently making, especially in the arena of public policy.

    That is why books like this one are so important. Through the eyes of over fifty young scholars from around the world, who participated in the 2017 Asia Leadership Treks (ALT) and met with thought-leaders and decision-makers from the realms of politics and government, business, community, and education, this fourth volume of *Rethinking Asia* showcases how Asia is dealing with its burgeoning influence through back-end stories, discussions, and policy-making structures. In addition to these enlightening meetings, visits to historical and cultural sites make the ALT an essential tool for exploring underlying trends and future directions in a range of Asian countries.

    Led by President Hungsoo S. Kim and Program Head John Lim, the ALT is a unique experience, enabling the Trekkers both to learn from Asian leaders and to share their own ideas. For four weeks in January 2017, one group met with movers and shakers in Yangon, Ho Chi Minh City, Hanoi, Jakarta, Penang, Kuala Lumpur, Seoul, and Tokyo. In June 2017, another group trekked through Manila, Hong Kong, Shanghai, Kuala Lumpur, Singapore, and Dhaka. The Treks' vigorous frameworks span the topics of entrepreneurship, leadership, innovation, and education, creating substantial analytical fodder for the Trekkers, who work in such diverse areas as medicine, academia, government, education, law, and international organizations and non-profits. Many of them go on to apply the best practices they have learned on the Trek to their own areas of expertise in their own countries.

In addition to the ALT, Hungsoo also runs the Asia Leadership Institute (ALI), both initiatives of his larger Center for Asia Leadership Initiatives (CALI). As a supplement to the Treks, several students—from Harvard's Schools of Government, Education, and Public Health, as well as Tufts' Fletcher School of Law and Diplomacy and even Imperial College London—were invited to participate as Teaching Fellows, mentors, and facilitators in the ALI's schools, camps, and conferences. These programs brought the students into close contact with Asia's most talented and aspiring leaders via Harvard-inspired coursework, TED-style talks, panel discussions, career mentoring, and seminars on professional skills, all designed to teach the participants how to make a positive impact in their communities.

The culmination of these experiences has been the creation of this book, a collection of essays written from different perspectives about different parts of Asia. The book—aptly named *Why Asia is Hopeful*—is divided into two sections: the ALT essays, in which the Trekkers describe their individual learning experiences and offer analyses of a range of countries and topics, and the ALI essays, in which the scholars who served as Teaching Fellows discuss their experiences in mentoring aspiring Asian leaders, from high-school students to mid-career executives.

I hope readers enjoy the essays as much as I did and, through them, gain the understanding they need to make their own decisions on how Asia is managing its vibrant growth while ensuring that its citizens adapt in these rapidly changing times. The book offers more than just fresh perspectives from the world's most renowned institutions; it also provides tangible insights from the policy-makers who have brought Asia to where it is today.

Steve Jarding
Lecturer in Public Policy
Harvard Kennedy School

Introduction

| Introduction |
Leading the Growth of Leadership Education in Asia

Hungsoo S. Kim, Editor
MPA, Harvard Kennedy School of Government

●●●

April 2018 marked the third anniversary of the Center for Asia Leadership Initiatives, or CALI, an organization I co-founded and currently lead. Upon returning from a month-long, eight-city, six-country Asia Leadership Trek in January 2017, I transitioned straight into reflection mode. I needed this because it had been some time since I had had time for myself, apart from my family and my work. Yes, the past three years—or five years altogether, including my two years at Harvard—had been hectic.

CALI's set-up preceded my graduation by only a month. I was keen to embark on this new journey, though I was unfamiliar with almost every aspect of it. In fact, I had every reason to call this "a journey in an uncharted territory," because I knew only a limited amount about the fields that my new work was bringing me into: education and leadership. Moreover, it was meant to be a social-profit endeavor. Rather than being a for-profit company, its aims were to advance public interest, to pioneer new ways of thinking, and to create a demand for what we thought would be meaningful and worthwhile to the community. Frankly speaking, from the business perspective, we had no sensible model, to begin with. But, nevertheless, I was ready to embark on an interesting adventure and knew that I could expect a lot of excitement in the future.

From the very start, I had to be comfortable with uncertainty and surprises. I also had to get used to wearing many different hats. At times, the work required me to work on tedious tasks like making hotel reservations for twenty rooms in each of seven cities, or booking air tickets that required twelve departures and landings for over forty individuals. At other times, I had to complete important, thought-intensive tasks like drafting a speech for a thousand-person audience at a leadership conference, formulating a strategy to spread the business into new areas, or leading delegations to meet with corporate and political leaders.

During the Treks, I encountered several challenges a day—from minor crises like people getting food-poisoning or missing a flight, to more major obstacles, such as held up at immigration or a chartered flight being called off just a few days before departure. All the while, I had to manage the expectations of the people at Harvard, as well as others.

These responsibilities required my immediate attention and action. The personal aspect of the new job by contrast, was more difficult to comprehend. I had three children to raise, no stable income for two straight years, no clear long-term prospect for where this endeavor would take us, and no immediate benefits at hand. I was at a constant battle with myself as to how I should steer the way forward. Looking back today, four years after CALI's inception, I see that there were overwhelmingly more things to be grateful for than not. The wisdom, knowledge, and friends I gained are irreplaceable. All in all, it was an unforgettable experience that I enjoyed despite all the stressful moments. Besides becoming a more mature human being, I was able to develop more awareness of both myself and society, and developed a systematic way of thinking through when attending to the many matters that required my focus and attention.

For these gifts, I give much credit to the original Asia Leadership Trek (ALT), an initiative that began at the Harvard Kennedy School (HKS) in March of 2012 when I traveled with thirty of my close colleagues to Korea to learn and be inspired. From there it became a platform to provide graduate students with a one-of-a-kind socio-economic and political study experience, and a community-service journey to Asia. Today, the Trek has grown to encompass nearly 350 scholars from 17 schools, including Harvard, MIT, Stanford, Columbia, and Tufts from over 86 nations.

The program has taken us to 68 locations in 26 countries in Asia; it has allowed us to meet with over 5,000 individuals and organizations; and it has given us the opportunity to engage and support 25,000 bright minds in Asia in over 60 leadership conferences that we have organized. For me, one word encapsulate all these experiences: humbling.

I have been thrilled to know many agents of change in an array of different countries, who are creating positive disruptions to make our world a better place. They are enacting their values in the lives they lead and the words they speak. Many of them are making improvements in other people's lives even under harsh circumstances or poor conditions. Despite not knowing what tomorrow holds for them, they work eagerly and diligently to increase the amount of hope in our world. Seeing what they had already accomplished humbled me, but also inspired me to join their efforts at improving our societies.

Here are a few examples of hope: a Nepalese woman running an NGO to save young women from being sold to brothels in India; a Malaysian tycoon who built one of the most well-respected business empires, donating his wealth to provide high-quality education for the young people of his nation; former guerrilla leaders in Myanmar who were in the war-zone for over two decades, now working toward the integration of the country's communities; a Cambodian-holocaust survivor running an educational organization to stanch the wounds of the past through education; a Filipino activist who played an instrumental role to restore the country's democratic rule of law by ousting long-time dictator Marcos; a renowned Kyrgyz entrepreneur helping the public transition from the old Soviet communist mentality to one dictated by the free market and democratic governance; a Korean technocrat helping the country navigate through new industrial policies so that it could rise out of abject poverty into an admirable state of development; a Thai educationist promoting education on financial inclusiveness for families from underprivileged backgrounds as a way to create opportunities for their future; one of the richest oligarchs in Kazakhstan, who built his way back up after being stripped of all his wealth in a political feud, now running his business solely for the good of the community. The list goes on and on.

Meeting these people and many others over the course of nearly four years bolstered my sense of responsibility and my commitment to the social cause—in particular education and leadership, which I see as the two key challenges in Asia. If we are to bring about fundamental changes in the public's perceptions and practices, both these require immense attention and intervention. In the end, this was the key benefit for me in my role in the ALT: finding my calling to pursue this cause.

*

Every generation has both the opportunity and the responsibility to meet the challenges of its era. The greatest issues confronting Asia today are regional security, an economic slowdown, racial tension, widening income gaps, and the digital divide. These problems are extremely complex, and yet they need to be urgently addressed. From my perspective, the root in solving them lies in the education and leadership training that the public receives. If the public education system can equip a nation's public with a creative, problem-solving mind-set, skills to initiate effective teamwork initiative to project a forward-thinking visions and a well-structured plan, then there is a far greater chance a nation can mitigate the impact of these problems. Moreover, if a community has well-respected leaders whom the public trusts, who warmly invite the public to work on challenges with them and who implement bold new actions that generate meaningful results, then the community will be in better hands against the problems that is facing us today. Finally, if the public possesses the leadership capacities needed to generate progress by discarding negative assumptions and adopting new, creative approaches to help chart a fresh course for their countries, then their communities will grow stronger and healthier.

Dedicated to these endeavors are the Asia Leadership Institute and the Acumen Case Center, two offshoots of the Asia Leadership Trek. The former was established in June 2014 to address the leadership challenges in Asia by equipping youth, professionals, managers, and officials from the government sector, civil society, and businesses throughout Asia with the knowledge, skills, and mind-sets required to face challenges and advance the public interests. About twenty-five programs have been developed so far to help individuals and organizations to make a difference by training them to go beyond their comfort zones. Through the programs, we also invite and mobilize diverse stakeholders to participate in making progress, and generate responses and solutions that produce shared values and outcomes. Thus far, the Institute prides itself on having organized over 100 events in over 50 cities in 24 countries.

The Acumen Case Center established in 2015, addresses the educational challenges in Asia. It engages in three important tasks: educator training, content research and development, and publishing. For the first two, the Center offers programs and materials that counter the transmission-heavy, rote-based model of education prevalent in Asia. The Center trains educators looking for novel, proven theories in the science of teaching, who wish to raise their teaching capacity and create a culture for innovative entrepreneurial teaching practices. To complete this aim the Center promotes two methods of teaching and learning: the Case Method, widely employed at Harvard University, and the Harkness Method, used by many renowned secondary schools across the U.S. The Center's Pedagogy Training Program both supplements institutional efforts to prepare individuals for the demands of a creative knowledge economy and trains decision-makers to formulate better education policies.

In November 2016, the ACC set up its Creativity & Breakthrough Initiative to develop a comprehensive collection of teaching materials, cases, and exercises on compelling topics from Asia, covering a wide range of issues from corporate, non-profit, community development, and ethics areas. These innovative teaching materials will assist in unlocking the creative potential of both individuals and teams; restructure groups to maximize each person's potential; teach individuals to communicate and advocate for change persuasively; and create a positive and supportive team culture. Participants will enhance their abilities to develop higher-order thought processes. Groups will discover that building high-impact teams improves their performances and outcomes.

Lastly, the Center's Acumen Publishing house offers a platform for ground-breaking ideas, provide strong guiding expertise, disseminates insightful analyses, and brings coaching to a diverse range of audiences in Asia and beyond. The publishing branch of the ACC covers general publications, including books and reflection pieces; content development, in which we develop course books and other materials for learning and teaching, both online and offline; alumni management, provide alumni with regular updates, new materials, and training for continuous growth and development; and, video production, which includes documentaries and video-based lectures.

As you can see, the ongoing legacy of the Asia Leadership Trek is truly momentous. At CALI we believe that any solutions for the challenges in Asia should begin with the foundational elements of education and leadership, as the best means of re-establishing, redefining, and realigning Asia's future towards what is in its and the world's best interest. In the future, education and leadership will certainly be the most important components for the Asian continent, as it has already become a hotbed of industrial innovation and dramatic social and cultural developments. We will need many leaders capable of inventing a new future for Asia that is purposeful and carefully planned, by locating windows of opportunities and by turning downsides into upsides. With the unprecedented rate of compressed growth that many communities in Asia are currently undergoing, and with the Fourth Industrial Revolution rapidly changing our society, I hope all our readers will see how important and urgent it is for us to train effective and ethical Asian individuals, who are educated and equipped with 21st-century skills and attributes.

In this Introduction, I have shared my leadership journey from the birth of the Asia Leadership Trek. What about the stories of others who have joined the Treks? Judging from the countless conversations I have had with fellow Trekkers, they also equally have compelling and breath-taking stories. Their testimonies show that the ALT has had an immense impact in many people's career trajectories and understanding of the world. Most important of all, the majority of the Trekkers say that they feel more connected to Asia after these experiences. They are now dedicated scholars, accomplished businessmen, legislators, corporate executives, social entrepreneurs, and educators; a sizable number of them are even actively engaged in affairs related to Asia, with a mission to bring Asia and the rest of the world closer together. They have told me how the ALT taught them to think deeply and broadly about both the successes and challenges of Asia and the impact that decisions and policies have on communities, markets, and institutions. Some have applied the invaluable lessons and practices they have learned through their work in other parts of the world.

One trekker, an American and a graduate of the HKS, joined the State Department after her Trek journey to play a greater role in creating shared values and understanding among nations. A Vietnamese Trekker with a degree from the Fletcher School, initiated an educational non-profit in Kathmandu to teach entrepreneurship skills to youths in Nepal, Bhutan, and Bangladesh. A British Trekker who graduated from the HBS, relocated to Asia as a professor, educating up-and-coming political leaders committed to advancing public interest. A Moroccan Trekker from the HKS, with an extensive background in international development now works to channel best practices into rural community development in Korea and Japan. This list of the Treks' impact is unending. Just imagine, every one of our 380 trekkers has a powerful story, and added to that are the stories of 30,000 conference participants across 26 countries in Asia that the Trekkers themselves have served.

The incredible journey that I began with the start of the ALT continues to go on with much excitement. CALI, an overarching body comprising three small projects, ALT among them, now operates in two main locations: Boston and Kuala Lumpur in Malaysia, with additional presences in Seoul, Tokyo, and Manila. The ten full-time staff-members, interns, and volunteers, along with over 60 country advisors, many of whom are graduates of the HKS and former Trek participants, work together with optimism and excitement to fulfill our long-standing commitment to Asia.

As part of that endeavor, I am delighted to present ALT's fourth publication. I am grateful to be able to introduce nine more insightful accounts by Trekkers and Teaching Fellows who took part in the

2017 Treks and Teaching Fellowship Programs, traveling to a total of 14 cities in 11 countries. I am honored to have worked with these ten contributors, exchanging ideas about their essays on some of the most valuable lessons they garnered from the Treks. It wasn't an easy task for any of them to take time out of our busy schedules to reflect, document, and produce these fine pieces of work. As I helped them prepare and edit their essays, I found great joy in getting to know them more deeply and increasing my own knowledge and understanding through their stories and insights.

Before I conclude, I want to revert to some thoughts I had after the January 2017 Trek. The two questions I mused over were "What more can we do to increase the value of the ALT and its many offshoots?" and "What will our efforts look like five to ten years from now?" The past three years have focused on exploration, expansion, and learning—pushing our boundaries, identifying opportunities for adding value to our communities, seeing how far we could go sustainably, and gaining expertise in the social-profit sector. I felt it was time to move up the value chain: consolidating our efforts in niche areas, ensuring that we were effective and efficient in what we did, and building our reputation in order to continue carrying out our vision, mission, and values. I pondered especially how best to leverage the different facets of the network we had built globally and regionally over the years, with the 450 Trekkers, 5,000 thought-leaders in Asia, and 30,000 program beneficiaries, as well as the 140 key stakeholders with whom we regularly collaborate with.

Since then, we have made great progress. Questions, failures, and experimentations have kept us focused. We are working hand in hand and have made many valuable improvements. Our mission to do real good has been renewed and reinvented. As I finish off this introduction, the fifth publication in the ALT series has already begun to take shape. I am looking forward to seeing what more there is to come and eagerly await the many new experiences that awaits us, humbling and inspiring. There will be more insightful stories and lessons to share, more creative people to meet, and more organizations making innovative and important changes around the world to partner with I believe.

Having now visited over half of the countries in the Asian continent—28 of the 48—the ALT will continue until we have visited all. I have spent much time this year reconnecting with friends in various locations that we will soon visit, including Lebanon, the United Arab Emirates, Israel, Georgia, Armenia, and Azerbaijan. My utmost wish is that our endeavor to connect communities within and beyond Asia will help to increase the effective leadership that we want to see in this world, by learning from and collaborating with one another. I humbly invite everyone, including all our authors, to benefit from what is shared in this book. I hope the stories will keep you warm, inspired, and thrilled. Enjoy!

Hungsoo S. Kim
President, Asia Leadership Trek
Center for Asia Leadership Initiatives

Part 1

Fellowship Essays

| Chapter 1 |
Reflections on Design Thinking in Asia

Helen van Baal
MA, Royal College of Art
MSC, Imperial College London

• • •

Kick-Off in Korea

"Hands up if you've heard of Design Thinking before."

I was looking at thirty-eight curious and very awake pairs of eyes. The room was quiet, there was tension in the air, but a good kind of tension. One that makes an educator feel that there's an expectation to deliver high-quality content, and when that happens the audience would take to heart what you are saying. Everyone was there, present and paid attention.

We had arrived in Seoul the day before, on a night flight. I had wanted to sleep during the day, but there was lots to prepare for the workshop I had to run. A tiring morning paired with a lack of sleep, On top of the lack of sleep, I was exhausted from the three previous weeks of traveling, facilitating workshops, and giving talks at conferences attended by over 3,000 people. My brain was barely awake. However, the second I walked into the classroom with thirty-eight young students, who came from eight countries across Asia, I realized that it going to be alright. Maybe it was the sense of expectation and anticipation in the room or a sense of being in the right place at the right time. These talented and committed students had convened to explore new thoughts, new ideas, and possibly life-changing experiences. In that brief moment before I kicked off the workshop, all the tiredness fell away, as if it had never existed.

However, and not surprisingly the beginning lacked engagement.

I have now lived and worked in seven different countries in Asia: China, Japan, Singapore, Malaysia, South Korea, Thailand, and the Philippines. In each one I either taught or facilitated design workshops. While working as a service designer for a large telecommunications company in Germany. I had stumbled upon Design Thinking (DT) before it became the buzzword it is today. After working as a program lead at the HPI Design School in Germany for several years thereafter, I started teaching it outside of the School. In the beginning, I worked with large corporations in Germany because they recognized the need for innovation and digital transformation. A few years later, DT had spread beyond the Stanford and HPI boundaries, and I found myself not only consulting for large companies, but working with SMEs, social enterprises, and educational institutions in a global setting.

During one of my first international projects, in collaboration with a university in China, I realized how much cultural context affects the creative process and how, both the process and the mindset in DT need to adapt to the culture it is applied in. Since DT is largely based on human-centered design, the user of a product or service plays an essential role in the process. Thus, obviously, the cultural context has an immense impact on the process itself. Observing these differences, both subtle and substantial in how DT is received, accepted, understood, misunderstood, interpreted, rejected, and implemented in different regions of the world became the focus of my work. As an educator and consultant, I started experimenting and adapting the processes and tools I was teaching depending on where I was and who I was working with. In my essay, I would like to present some of my observations, experiences, and insights from teaching DT in different countries in Asia.

The Asia Union Leadership Summit (AULS) program in Seoul, was one of the many programs in which I taught DT during my summer fellowship at the Center for Asia Leadership Initiatives (CALI). Apart from South Korea, we also ran conferences and programs in Malaysia, China, and the Philippines: these were The Asia Leadership Youth Camp and Executive Leadership School, China Emerging Leadership Initiative, and Mobilizing Teams for Change: Tools and Mindset.

What Is Design Thinking and Why Is It Relevant in a Leadership Context?

When I first heard of the AULS, I suspected that the programs would revolve around topics like "leadership strategies," "essential skills for emerging leaders," or maybe "becoming a successful leader." Instead, the CALI team and I chose to make DT the core of the program. Since in Asia "design" is often considered "fun but unprofitable" or "creative but not important," this was a bold move. It not only showed how forward-thinking CALI's leadership training was but it directly impacted many of our delegates' careers and lives as I saw. So what *is* DT? Essentially, DT applies the tools and phases of the design process to complex or "wicked" problems and innovative challenges.

Often, when we think of design, we think of fashion design or graphic design, and we associate the word with something superficial such as trying to make a product or interface *look pretty*. The design I refer is holistic and structured to fulfill problem solving needs. For example, it could be the design of a new prosthetic leg that is affordable, sustainable, and accessible for amputees living in rural Africa, or the design of new government services that create a simple and human-centric experience for citizens, visitors, and refugees.

Nevertheless, the process in any type of design is quite similar. Whether you are designing a new chair or a way for individuals to rent out their flats, you will have to go through the following steps: *Research*. Who are you designing for? A young family living in the suburbs of New York or a single elderly lady living in rural Germany? What are their needs, values, and daily routines? Then you focus or define a *Point of View*. What unique insight are you basing your design on? This insight should be very specific and is often an underlying need rather than an obvious wish. Next you start creating ideas—the *Ideation* or idea-generation phase. Ideally you come up with a range of different ideas, often using various brainstorming techniques. After selecting a few ideas, you test them out by building quick Prototypes. *Prototypes* help to refine an idea, to test it with your audience, and to go from the abstract to the concrete. What does it feel like to use this interface? Would people want to rent out their apartments to strangers, and, if so, what does the experience of using the app or website feel like? How does the prosthesis fit? Can users fit it by themselves, or will they need support? After *Testing* the prototypes and absorbing the feedback, you *Iterate* and improve your design.

Depending on the type of design you are working on, different parameters may come into play. When designing products, for instance, the production process, materials, and regulations need to be considered. When designing for the web or social media, timing, and devices play an essential role. When designing services or systems, the user experience and all of the touch points between your design and your users need to be designed. The rough process, however, will still involve these fundamental design steps: research, define, ideate, prototype, and test. In addition to the process itself, there is a certain mindset or work mode that design work often demands: working in multidisciplinary teams, going through quick iterations, and focusing on human needs and a visual, hands-on approach.

DT takes these ingredients (the process and the mindset) and puts them into the hands of non-designers or multidisciplinary teams consisting of both designers and non-designers. It applies the ingredients to projects that are not necessarily considered within the traditional design disciplines. You might use the process to improve the arrival process for refugees, or to redesign the security control at an international airports, or to design ways to sterilize medical equipment in hospitals without reliable electricity. Making use of the human-centered approach and the creative and iterative methods by which designers navigate complexity and uncertainty, we can now empower non-designers to tackle larger and more complex challenges.

Why place DT at the core of leadership trainings? To answer this question, let's go back to the morning I kicked off the workshop in Seoul. After a brief introduction, I asked the students to find their teams and start unpacking the design challenge I had posed for them. The first tension now transformed into excitement. I had given them a big and complex challenge to solve: how would they redesign cross-national collaboration in Asia, taking history and traditional barriers into consideration? The project had no easy answer; it would be challenging to solve it in just four days; yet it was very relevant to each of their realities. I had thought about this carefully and had deliberately chosen a topic that they could relate to but that would force them to leave their comfort zones and open up to each other. In a short amount of time, they would have to learn as much as possible about each other's cultures and would need to look at the historical developments of the region they lived in while figuring out how to shape and create a better future. Though they didn't realize it, I had given them a job that many of them would face in the future: creating a collaborative, fair, and progressive Asia. Plus, I was giving them the tools and framework to not only think about this but to create and design real solutions.

Teams started to form, introductions were made in the groups, chairs moved around, and the first mind-maps of ideas and associations started appearing on whiteboards. This was good—they had accepted the challenge and were ready to give it their best.

Now their goal was to identify a sub-topic that the team wanted to focus on. Some chose to work on cultural understanding between countries, while others focused on ways to foster cross-national collaboration, such as travel apps for tourists. Some teams were interested in more specific problems, such as gender equality and language barriers. To get an idea of how each of the teams were doing, I moved around, observing team dynamics, listening to their first ideas, and throwing in the occasional hint or prompt.

By the time I finished my round, I realized that one of the teams had stopped writing on the whiteboard and looked frustrated. "What have you found so far?" I asked. One of the girls in the group—let's call her Lina—seemed upset. "How do we know what topic to focus on?" she asked, and added, "There are so many. Which one is correct?"

Even though this particular team was stuck while all of the others were moving forward, they had identified one of the key characteristics of design challenges—ambiguity. A design challenge doesn't have a correct answer. There's no right or wrong path. Instead, design provides you with a methodology to navigate complexity and ambiguity. In a world where problems are no longer straightforward, where technology is exponentially evolving, and where people, structures, and communication are accelerating and getting more interconnected, there are no right answers anymore.

The new generation of leaders will need a new set of skills, and DT is one way of acquiring and strengthening those skills. Not only through textbooks but also through hands-on, experiential, and real-world exposure and application. Apart from dealing with ambiguity, DT helps strengthen people's ability to empathize and collaborate with others, deal with uncertainty and complexity, develop creative confidence, and learn from mistakes. By working on real design challenges, you learn to understand the nature of a problem, grasp its dimensions, and generate ideas and solutions. Through this process, you don't only "solve" a complex problem, but you also learn how to navigate multidisciplinary approaches, practice collaboration, and build creative stamina. These are essential skills for every leader to have in the 21st century. These skills are difficult to acquire just by reading about them. By experiencing them firsthand, they enable you not only to handle ambiguity but to grow into a better person and a leader.

Reflections on Teaching Design Thinking in Asia

In the next few pages, I would like to share some of my key takeaways and thoughts from teaching design and DT in Asia to an Asian audience, focusing on which parts of the design process were difficult and easy for students to learn, and which parts I as an instructor did well or struggled with. There were a few surprising findings.

Before going into the details, I would like to clarify that this discussion is subjective and based on specific encounters and situations. That's what makes the lessons tangible and real, but they are not the only truth. In addition, since the countries and regions I have visited are unique, my takeaways may not fit into all contexts. The following table encapsulates this thought:

What this is:
- Lessons from my own experience of teaching DT in Asia
- Individual stories and impressions
- Reflections on the design process in different cultures in Asia

What this is not:
- Based on quantitative research
- A guideline of how DT should be taught
- Only applicable to Asia
- Trying to sell DT as a magic wonder tool that will solve all your (innovation) problems

• *Takeaway #1: Creative Problem-Solving Requires the Unlearning of Traditional Problem-solving Techniques*

When Lina's team started to work on their first design challenge, they struggled with how to approach it. When they realized that it was up to them to define their own path, without having a clear goal, they felt nervous and hesitant to continue. Over the past five years, I've encountered this situation in many different contexts, from senior managers in Europe to university students in Africa. However, when working with high-school and undergraduate students in Asia, the fear of approaching challenges that don't have a "correct" answer seemed more prominent, compared to students in the West. One possible explanation to this is the way Asian school systems are structured and incentivized. While both Eastern and Western schools still heavily rely on individual grading systems, in Asia the pressure for doing well in exams is much greater and is often increased by both parents and teachers. There is nothing wrong with doing well in school and working hard to get good grades, but skills that require more time and are harder to evaluate, such as creativity and collaboration, are often left out of the curriculum. Ironically, and due to the fact that many Asian countries are rapidly changing, driven by technological as well as economic progress, it is exactly these skills that are becoming more important.

After working with different age groups in various countries in Asia, I learned this crucial point: the earlier these skills can be learned, the better! Lina was about to enter college when I met her in Seoul, and her experiences in high school had taught her a certain way of thinking and approaching problems. Learning to tackle challenges in new ways was demanding for her because it meant letting go of her old ways of problem-solving. Yet she remained open and engaged, and over the course of the next few days she became one of the students who impressed me the most. On the final day of the program, she approached me and said, "Miss Helen, this was really hard!" She looked tired, but in her eyes I saw a glimmer of triumph. She had managed to internalize a new way of thinking and working, a skill that gets harder and rarer as we grow older. During those few days of intense workshops, I had managed to push her far enough (but not too far) out of her comfort zone for her to learn, grow, and challenge herself. Later, about a week after the program in Seoul, I received an email from her, asking me for feedback on the new game app she was developing and input on how to structure the design process.

While seventeen-year-old Lina is still able and willing to change her ways of thinking, many working professionals have gotten so used to their methods of approaching challenges that it takes much more than just a few days to introduce new problem-solving skills to them. In a rapidly changing society, it is necessary but takes a lot of hard work and patience to unlearn our old ways of thinking in order to make room for new, open-minded, and creative methods of problem-solving. These skills offer a valuable opportunity, a chance not only to keep up with change but to design and shape it as well.

• *Takeaway #2: Building Creative Confidence Also Means Building Personality*

What I love most about my job is seeing young people grow and guiding them to become more confident, creative, and passionate individuals. At the AULS, I was very fortunate to work with some of the most intelligent, courageous, and passionate young people I have ever met. Even though we had only a few days of workshops and lectures, working with a group like that allowed me to push far beyond the standard DT workshop.

This boundary-pushing manifested itself in two ways. First, it happened on a content level, teams developed feasible product ideas with fleshed-out business models in only a few days. Second, on a much larger scale, there was a shift in the students' mindset and approach toward a more open, more innovative, and more creative way of working. The prerequisite for this mindset is building a safe space, where students are comfortable with allowing their ideas to fail, by making mistakes and learning from them.

Oscar was one of the youngest students in the group, and one of the loudest. He knew he was smart, and he was constantly looking for ways to be one step ahead of everyone else. At various points in the process, I asked each team to partner with another team, pitch their ideas, and receive feedback. Often, when students are asked to do that for the first time, their pitch becomes a sales pitch where they want to make sure the other team likes their idea. It usually takes a few rounds of sharing for teams to understand that it is much more valuable for them to receive constructive feedback than to convince others of their idea.

On day two, it was Oscar's turn to share an idea with a partner team. There hadn't really been enough time to prepare for this pitch, but Oscar was confident that he could improvise and convince everybody of their ingenious idea. Nevertheless, the pitch didn't go well and the other team, prompted to give feedback, questioned some of the core aspects of the game that Oscar's team had come up with. At the end of the workshop, when all the other students had left for dinner, an unusually quiet Oscar stayed behind. "I'm sorry our presentation wasn't good, Miss Helen," he said, shuffling his feet. I smiled and explained that the aim of the presentation wasn't to showcase the idea but to find ways of improving it. I reminded him that his team had learned a lot from the presentation. His face lightened. "So we did well by not doing well?" He said that as if a weight had been lifted off his shoulders.

For me, this was a powerful moment: I was able to take some of the pressure off him and let him to allow himself to make mistakes. Later on, this led to his whole team developing a certain lightness, which reflected in a sensible and well-thought-out idea. One that didn't need a great sales pitch but won over their audience naturally, thanks to their hard work and the genuine feedback they received from testing it with others. Of course, the idea itself wasn't what I was proud of—what pleased me was the mindset and attitude that the team had adopted.

Allowing yourself to make mistakes is a skill that takes a lot of confidence and courage, but it also will help you grow into a better designer, better leader, and better individual. The idea of "doing well by not doing well" is the first lesson that any educational system should convey. Unfortunately, in many educational institutions, especially in Asia, embracing this idea will require a lot of work and a dramatic change in mindset.

• *Takeaway #3: When it Comes to Innovation, Teenagers Are One Step Ahead of CEOs*

Innovation means discovering problems that haven't been addressed yet and then creating solutions that have never existed before. This requires openness. Openness to doing things differently and to change a process or product, and also openness in approach and attitude. For new technology, the two extremes of this attitude are represented by the "innovators" or tech enthusiasts on the one hand, and by the "laggards" or skeptics on the other. In production, similarly, you have innovators (companies that are constantly pushing innovation, and create new products and services) and laggards (companies in more traditional disciplines, that are not necessarily forced to innovate to survive).

DT enables innovation. In order to unleash this potential, however, you need to do more than simply apply the process step by step; you need to be open to the change that innovation and working innovatively entail. The level of openness is often directly reflected in the way that participants in DT workshops adopt to new processes and tools. In order to be innovative or to create innovation, the laggards need to move toward the innovators, and that can sometimes be challenging, especially once you've gotten used to a certain way of working.

All of our participants at the AULS were highly savvy and smart, interested in matters of policy, history, and technology. There was so much enthusiasm for learning. When learning new concepts, thinking creatively, and adopting new processes, these teenagers were open to the new and different, and that placed them one step ahead of most of the professionals I had previously worked with.

I've led many DT workshops over the course of the past seven years, with participants ranging from elementary-school kids to top management (mostly the latter). Some of these workshops ran smoothly; the teams understood and were able to apply the tools straight away. Usually these workshops were fun, because the process allows the teams not only to play with ideas and create innovative solutions but to push the boundaries of DT as a framework and mindset. As a result, they developed a team culture and worked in a flow. Then there are the other workshops, those that are challenging, especially in the beginning, because there were resistance to the process and a "this-is-not-how-we-do-things" skepticism. This doesn't happen so much with elementary-school kids but frequently occurs with top management. Such workshops require more work from the instructors' side, as we convince people to be open to the process. The upside is that once these skeptical participants do open up, you can often have a much greater impact on them and the way they work. You can actually create a more innovative working culture in a company or persuade senior management to invest time and money into innovation, where before there was no understanding of a process that doesn't necessarily have a clear and direct output but that requires time to understand. Eventually, they come to understand the benefits of creating a range of possible solutions and not just running with the first one.

At the AULS, the talented young delegates taught me that there is a third kind of workshop, one that combines the best of both worlds: an open and accepting mindset and a critical and healthy questioning of both the topic and the approach itself. I have rarely experienced such a highly intellectual approach to DT or such a playful and collaborative attitude. Many of the top managements people I have worked with could have learned a lot from those teenagers.

- *Takeaways #4: Leaders Must Be Value-Creators*

The Executive Leadership School was a program that we ran in Kuala Lumpur. Working professionals of diverse industries and ranks came together to take a deep dive into what leadership means in today's context and why it was so important that we formed a new understanding and practice of it, especially in our personal and organizational settings. What I liked about this program was that the participants came equipped with rich experience, expertise, and lessons to share.

For the ELS, my colleague Craig Brimhall and I designed a workshop that combined elements of DT with the concept of embracing diversity. Initially, we had planned to conduct two separate workshops, but we soon realized that we might both benefit if we combined them and approached the more abstract topic of diversity in an applied DT way. We set up the room so that the participants had to divide into four teams. As this was a new format, we were excited and enjoyed designing it. At the same time, I was a little nervous because of my previous experience working with executives, who were skeptical and resistant. I knew it would take convincing arguments to get the teams to leave their comfort zone and start exploring previously unthinkable ideas—not to mention the difficulty of persuading these experienced professionals to build prototypes out of play-dough and pipe cleaners.

A few days into the workshop, we knew it was going well. Craig and I were learning a lot, and the participants were interested and exploring both DT and diversity in new ways. By introducing new tools, playing warm-up games, and prompting quick, unprepared presentations, we were gently pushing them out of their comfort zone.

Finally, we got to the prototyping phase. This phase was the hardest for people who were used to creating value through long discussions, PowerPoints, and sitting around meeting-room tables. I had prepared my arguments carefully and revisited them again just before my introduction to prototyping. I emphasized that this stage allows you to learn and to make mistakes early on, which eventually will save you time and money. I explained that because it allows you to communicate your idea and get real, valuable feedback, it helps to speed up your project.

When I finished my presentation, everyone immediately started getting material and building prototypes. Convincing them had been surprisingly easy. Usually, this was one of the hardest parts for me as a coach. I had been prepared to push the participants to leave their comfort zone, to coax them into making the transition from thinking and talking to making and building. Why was it easy this time around?

Stepping back, I observed the teams and quickly realized that there was a difference in the prevalent team dynamic, compared with other professional groups I had worked with. All of the teams at the ELS had a natural way of collaborating, which didn't involve much talking. Working with professionals in Europe and the U.S., I had often observed a reluctance to move from talking to making. Sometimes teams would even move back from the prototyping space to a table to continue debating their idea. Here in Asia, however, the teams seemed to work better and more constructively while building their prototypes. Even though their ideas weren't mature yet—prototyping can be a powerful tool to develop an idea as well as to visualize it. The teams seemed confident in building them.

While the ideation and synthesis phases often require decision-making and discussion, during prototyping a more fluid and organic interaction came into play. The team-members were still making decisions, but they did so by visualizing and, quite literally, building on each other's ideas. To some extent, I would argue that Eastern cultures were more comfortable with this way of working than Western cultures, which tend to be more comfortable in discussing and debating a focus point or idea.

A slightly more academic explanation can be drawn from military strategy. The classic Western approach can be traced back to Carl von Clausewitz (1780-1831) and his analysis *On War*, in which he describes military strategy as "planning followed by implementation." Given the rise of engineering and science in the nineteenth century, it is not surprising that this very technical framework found a large following in Europe after his death. But the Eastern approach to military strategy is very different. One of the most frequently cited sources, *The Art of War* by Sun Zi, a Chinese general from the 5th century BCE, describes thirty-six strategies that are not technical but are rather illustrations of behavioral opportunities.

At the ELS, I realized that the teams' approach to prototyping in DT was much closer to Sun Zi's take on strategy than to the Western way of planning first and executing afterwards. While it would be far too generalized to say that every professional in Europe or the West still follow von Clausewitz's technical approach to strategy, I was fascinated to discover that DT teams in the East clearly felt more comfortable working visually.

Regardless of the approach that you take as a leader, in the 21st century leadership means not only providing guidance and enabling others but also creating value. In our increasingly complex world, those who hold leadership positions must be able to both direct and to create. Providing solutions means being able to make and build them, not just discuss about them. A better word can only be created if all of our leaders understand this. As a designer, creating is inherent to my work and being, and I have found DT a good means of encouraging people in other disciplines to start creating as well.

That ease with which the ELS delegates approached prototyping is something I wished many Western executives could observe. By thinking with their hands, the teams didn't only achieve better outcomes and ideas; they also demonstrated problem-solving as an essential leadership skill.

- *Takeaway #5: Problem-Solving in the 21st Century Means Being Able to Iterate*

Partly because of the speed of the region's development, Asians tend to want immediate results. This is inherent in their education system and even more apparent in their work environments. DT, however, especially in the first half of the process, doesn't deliver fast results. On the contrary, it is an essential part of the process to meet your users, have long conversations, and learn about people's lives, thoughts, feelings, and needs. Only then can you create good, meaningful, human-centered solutions. This takes time, and—even more irritatingly, it requires you to take time for something you may not see the immediate value in. This can be frustrating, and many Asian organizations don't understand the benefit of spending money on such a process. To them, it feels counterintuitive.

Over the years and working in different contexts, I have developed some strategies and approaches for applying DT without committing to large-scale change or investment.

Strategy #1: Invest Only a Little Bit

What's the minimum time and money you are willing to invest? This can be for training or on a real project. By keeping investment low, both expectations and risk are kept to a minimum, which in turn allows for creativity and failure. We sometimes call this stage "the playground." There are no expectations of generating feasible results; if something valuable is created, then expectations are exceeded and a willingness to place more trust in the process is guaranteed in the next step.

Strategy #2: Prototype and Test It

Prototyping and testing a concept are essential steps in the design process. They should also be part of the implementation of DT in our organizations. Instead of changing the entire product-development process, for instance, try running part of the project using DT and the other part using your usual methods. Afterward, evaluate at what points in your process DT is beneficial. This way, you're taking minimal risk and implementing only those aspects of DT that benefit and suit the existing organizational structures. Additionally, this iterative way of implementing DT might lead to creating your own version of DT, which might be the more sustainable approach and be of value in itself.

Strategy #3: Fragment the Process
Instead of applying the full DT process and mindset to a project, department, or organization, break it up and start with the part that resonates most with the content of your work and the organizational culture. You should take into consideration your goals and expectations, your budget, your time restrictions, and the prevalent working attitude of your organization. Some starting points could be short brainstorming sessions, creating a more collaborative work space, or spending time doing user research at the beginning of a project.

Applying these strategies allows for flexibility and may lead gradually to changes that would otherwise require patience or leaps of faith. In effect, you will be introducing an iterative process in an iterative way.

- *Takeaway #6: Value the Essence of Diversity*

One of the core principles of DT is multidisciplinary learning. The multidisciplinary aspect of ELS came from the participants' different professional backgrounds, while at the AULS it manifested in the delegates' various nationalities. In order to embrace diversity and inclusivity, a collaborative mindset is needed. Working with DT in Asia is fascinating because of the region's richness in diversity. Every day I encountered different cultures, religions, traditions, and languages, and I found countless opportunities to learn from a wide array of perspectives. Yet, while harmonious communication and a rigorous work ethics are strongly emphasized, diversity and inclusion are often not directly addressed.

Diversity plays an important role in my work as an instructor, and there are two reasons for this. First, in our everyday work life there is often not enough time to address diversity directly and constructively. Second, DT is an excellent toolkit for navigating diversity. Empathy—the ability to see the world from someone else's perspective—is an essential part of the DT process, and collaboration in DT's multidisciplinary teams allows them to create better, more holistic solutions. These are only two examples of how we can instill an appreciation for diversity in organizations by using DT, as well as using DT to resolve any friction that may arise among diverse mindsets and backgrounds.

In the research phase at the AULS in Seoul, I asked the students to interview each other about their cultures, perceptions, and traditions. This gave the students an excuse to learn about each other on a deeper level and to strengthen their empathy. It also encouraged them to start rethinking their own perspectives. When I was reflecting on this afterwards with my colleagues, one of them said, "AULS was so great because we had so many different cultures in one room. Without that diversity, the learning wouldn't have been this rich." Looking back at it now, I think she was right. Learning is amplified by diverse perspectives, but accessing these perspectives is hard if you're surrounded by people with similar backgrounds and experiences.

This leads me to my second point: DT as a toolkit for navigating diversity. While diversity can enrich learning, it doesn't do this by itself; instead, in order for people to access, understand, and benefit from diversity, they must possess the right tools. DT provides those tools because it puts an emphasis on empathy, requires different skill sets, and is based on human needs. After both the AULS and the ELS, the participants mentioned that their way of seeing their fellow delegates had changed and impacted their own perspective. Asian countries are fortunate in having such diversity available to them, but the big challenge is to make good use of it. DT allows its users to learn from diversity, understand other perspectives, maintain rich cultures, and apply acquired knowledge to create better, more inclusive environments.

What's Next?

Continuing growth paired with increasing complexity means that there is a growing need for DT in Asia. The next challenge will be to create culturally appropriate versions of the DT tools and process. This is already happening at many institutions and locations across Asia, the Center for Asia Leadership being one of them. It is also necessary to ask more searching questions: How can the "Western" model of DT be adapted, complemented, extended, and integrated into different cultural contexts? When are new processes necessary and useful, and when are they needless or hindering? How can we transition from learning and adapting innovative working modes to defining and designing the future of leadership?

Living and working in Asia in the 21st century is fascinating, overwhelming, and incredibly enriching at the same time. I'm grateful to have had this experience and am looking forward to seeing the new generation of leaders have an impact in the world.

I started this chapter by sharing with you a moment from the first day of the AULS in Seoul. Let me end with a moment from the last day. After four intense days of workshops, very little sleep, and an exciting last day of final presentations and reflections, we were all gathered again in the same room where we had started our journey together. Everything was different through friendships had been made that would last a lifetime, and experiences had been lived through that would never be forgotten. There had been ups and downs, joy and tears. While some of this was because we had carefully selected the participants and created the right atmosphere for them to learn in, the intensity and growth that these students had experienced together was due to DT itself. The process had allowed them to open up to each other, to be vulnerable and make mistakes, to learn from these mistakes and grow, to play and to create. It had given them the space to gain creative confidence and to come together in teams and as a group. Equally importantly, it had given them the tools to practice good leadership in the 21st century.

It was time to say good-bye, and again there was tension in the room. This time it stemmed from gratitude, a fear of letting go, and the sense that this was just the beginning. We asked the students to share some of their favorite parts of the AULS, and one after another stood up, not only to share what they had learned but to show all of us that this experience had had an impact on their lives and would have an impact on the world. I knew then that leading the workshop had been worth the thousands of miles, many sleepless nights, and countless hours of work.

| Chapter 2 |

Topia:
Educating Young Leaders on Adaptive Leadership in Dynamic Asia

Ami Valdemoro

MPP, Harvard Kennedy School of Government

• • •

A long time ago, in a galaxy far, far away... I am a big fan of Star Wars. Maybe it was my older sister's influence on me—she introduced me to the franchise when I was seven or eight years old and she was fourteen. At first I thought she was crazy. Who were all of these men in plastic suits? Who was the tall guy with the deep, robotic voice? Why did the smallest of the creatures—a little green being with pointy ears—seem to be more powerful than the rest? As I learned more about the Jedi knights, I realized there might be something to all of this. It helped that the main characters in the end managed to defeat the Dark Side.

I often use the Jedi metaphor from Star Wars to explain the most important components of Adaptive Leadership to my classes, though I could also easily use a more modern-day reference, such as Harry

Potter or the Divergent series. At the start of my session, I tell the students that to exercise leadership, they need to train their mind, heart, guts, and spirit, just as a Jedi Warrior would. Like any skill, it is a practice—something you can excel at with time but perhaps never truly master.

I find that it helps to use popular-culture references when introducing a meta-concept like leadership, particularly in Asian contexts, where students are taught—conditioned—to take the teacher's word for it and aren't encouraged to think critically or differently. One of the characteristics of Asian cultures is deference to "elders"—teachers, grandparents, parents, older siblings, bosses. It is a tradition that dates back thousands of years and has allowed these cultures (and subcultures) to flourish over time. However, as we move further into the 21st century, this deference may hinder the capacity of Asian societies to be innovative and to address new challenges, whether they be poverty, unemployment, or natural disasters.

Part of my role as a Teaching Fellow in Adaptive Leadership is to help students unlearn some behaviors that have proven useful in the past but may be limiting in the future. In their place, I show the importance of knowing how to read a room and comprehend the roles they might play in that room. Understanding when an issue is hot and how to ripen an issue for discussion; developing the courage to ask questions, speak up, and call attention to things that don't seem right; knowing when some voices in a room are not being heard; and having the courage to empower others to learn, grow, and lead.

This essay is a reflection of my experience in teaching Adaptive Leadership to high-school students from eight different countries during the Asia Union Leadership Summit in Seoul, organized by the

Center for Asia Leadership in July 2017. The piece is structured on a few of the key components of the Adaptive Leadership framework and includes anecdotes to illustrate my impressions of the students and how they both understood and exercised leadership during our time together.

There is Madness in the Method *(Mind)*

When I teach Adaptive Leadership, I want to make sure that my students understand from the get-go how the tools they learn in class can be used to recognize opportunities to lead in their daily life. To do this, I use examples from familiar situations, like school or family, to deepen students' understanding of a key concept. Often I also use the "case-in-point" method, drawing upon what happens in the class itself to illustrate a learning point. This means that, as I teach concepts to the class and the students interact with one another, I observe what's going on in the room. Depending on the point I want to highlight, I'll jump in at certain moments or withdraw in others to help the students understand how people might act when they come together to work on something. The case-in-point method often confuses students at first, since it places me in the role of participant rather than teacher. At times, for example, I will sit down without warning in the middle of a lecture, to observe whether students will pick up a point that one of their classmates has brought up before we move on.

Before the Summit, while I knew that this way of teaching could be very effective, I worried about the effect that my unconventional methods might have in Asia. But I kept in mind the Skype conversation I had had with Mark, a teaching fellow from my Adaptive Leadership class and a community organizer, on a weekday afternoon in May. I was excited to get on the phone with him after weeks of scheduling issues, but I also felt a bit nervous. Could I do justice to the material that we usually covered in two full semesters of graduate school in five-day workshop modules?

"Your module looks really good—what are you concerned about?" Mark said matter-of-factly, sensing my hesitation through the pixelated video screen.

"Frankly, I'm worried that I won't be able to cover this material with enough depth, because they will be looking at me to provide the answers."

Mark stroked his beard. Then, an impish smile appeared on his face as he said, "Why don't you play on that, and put them in situations in which they have to resolve the issues on their own authority?"

That gentle nudge was all it took.

Ask What You Can Do *(Heart)*

The dates marking the start of my two-month fellowship journey inched closer and closer. I took pleasure in tearing out each successive page of my calendar, but I was growing anxious about the journey. I looked to people like Mark to comfort me in the face of my own uncertainties, but Mark refused to give me a simple answer. Instead, he turned the question back to me, so that I could figure out how to solve it on my own.

Eventually I realized that my anxiety about teaching leadership in Asia stemmed from my own personal journey and my previous wrestling with the subject. I am a Filipino American who grew up as a Third-Culture Kid, but I found myself living and working in Asia after graduating from university. Instinctively, I knew that things worked differently in Asia. In particular, the "Big Boss" mentality still existed in many countries in the region. Instead of having each team or group member contribute equal weight to a project or problem, whatever the Big Boss said goes. In other words, the boss' wishes have a greater weight than the opinions of everyone else on the team. This unequal power dynamic is not unique to Asia—I'd also seen it in my work in sub-Saharan Africa—but it does make teaching adaptive leadership a challenge. If people are used to social or cultural structures in which they don't feel that they can challenge the dominant authority, then how can they be empowered to exercise leadership? In spite of my natural ability to adapt to different contexts, I was worried that I wouldn't know how to use my intuition to help the students understand their own opportunities to exercise leadership.

From elementary school to high school, I lived mostly in the U.S. Even when I lived and studied in Mexico, I was encouraged to ask questions by the authority figures in my life. Speaking up was encouraged, especially if what I had to say would benefit my classmates. In the best of circumstances, teachers were my guides—not distant, infallible elders. That distinction was reserved for the teachers I could not connect with, or whose approaches to their roles made me feel both incompetent and incapable of asking them questions. I can remember the glint in Ms. Lawrence's eyes whenever I raised my hand in her sixth-grade history class. She knew—and I knew—that this might be the start of a great conversation. The practice of asking questions, not to undermine authority but to deepen my understanding, continued throughout my education, formal or otherwise. It became critical in college and graduate school. The motto of the Harvard Kennedy School (HKS), where I got my Master's degree, was "Ask what you can do." While we were expected to go out and "do" great things upon graduating, the emphasis during my two years in Cambridge was to "ask" as much as I could of my teachers, my classmates, and myself.

It was this process of asking that led me to the Summit. In my second year at HKS, I started exploring what kind of leadership it would take for our communities—local, national, and global—to address the most pressing challenges confronting us today and in the future: the spread of disease, the universal need for high-quality education, climate change, the dangers of incompetent governance. A foundational part of this journey was the Adaptive Leadership coursework I took in the fall and winter of 2012. In Ron Heifetz's class, I delved into leadership not just as a theory but as a practice, through cases that forced our class to find innovative solutions to real problems.

Ron required each of us to examine a specific leadership challenge that we had faced—usually in the professional sphere. He taught us, in diagnosing this challenge with our classmates, how to understand the constraints that limited our ability to be effective leaders. For example, were there external threats to our work or to our organization—anything from armed insurgents to a competitor working on a similar product? What about internally—were there people or groups within your area that could be threatened by the project you were working on, and who were critical to ensuring its success? By examining the ecosystems we worked in and reframing the challenges we faced, Ron helped us discover new options for how to exercise leadership in the future.

This is hard work. Recalling the journey now, even with five years' distance, makes my stomach churn. I've literally set aside the coffee that I'm drinking as I write this.

From the Balcony to the Dance Floor (*Gut*)

It was a cold, dreary winter evening in Cambridge, Massachusetts. At 5 p.m., when I walked back to my house from campus, it was nearly pitch black. I sat by the bay window of our beautiful third-floor apartment on Hingham Street, a pile of books and a generous glass of Pinot Noir in front of me. As I stared out into the gray, snowy haze and took another swig, I remembered how I had stocked up on wine at Trader Joe's the day before J-term (or winter-break) classes started. This was going to be a long two weeks. The bottle was already half-empty.

I needed to start writing my reflection paper for Ron's class, and I didn't know how to begin. To do this work properly, I had to open up some serious emotional and psychological scars. I would have to admit openly, to some of the brightest minds that I had ever met in my life, that I had failed—epically. For an over-achieving student at Harvard, this exercise sounded at best ego-bruising and at worst masochistic.

Like any good student, I began to procrastinate. I checked Instagram for photos of my friends' travels to warm, sunny oases—clearly they had made the right decision to leave Cambridge. I cleaned my apartment, even though my flatmates were gone for the month. Then, midway through mopping the dining-room area, I threw my hands in the air. Out loud, I shouted at anyone who was there to listen (just me), "Why does this matter? What's the big deal? Why do you care so much?"

Ron had told us to trust the process as we went through his two-week intensive course. This wasn't the last night that I questioned the process, myself, and just about everything else that could be questioned. Finally, out of the blue, on one of my long walks to and from campus, the answer to my question suddenly came to me. I realized that part of my fascination—or, dare I say it, obsession—with leadership was due in part to my cultural DNA. True, I wanted to understand what makes a good or bad leader. More than that, though, I wanted to know why certain societies were able to solve problems in their communities and why others can't seem to succeed. To be more specific, why can't the Philippines, once the Pearl of the Orient and a model emulated by countries like South Korea and Singapore, shake off its "Sick Man of Asia" reputation?

More questions poured out after this revelation. What can we learn from others as we face common challenges like poverty, sickness, and inequality? How can we work together with people from different contexts, backgrounds, and countries when our collective narratives paint others in an unflattering light? Why is it that in some places people welcome questions, whereas in others asking questions poses real risks?

By the time I finished my J-term class, I realized two things. First, asking questions is one of the most valuable practices of leadership. If I want to move a group of people from Point A to Point B, asking questions can help me understand how to guide them through that process. Just like my own journey in that snowy winter of 2013, it might be messy, and it might require them to give up some things. But asking questions will give me the information I need to help them through that discomfort. Second, the stream of questions I was asking myself compelled me in one direction—east. In examining my own leadership case, I realized that my future lay not in my past work as a public health advocate but in Asia. I owed it to myself to seek answers to the questions that surfaced on those cold nights. Why did so many people in my parents' generation leave the Philippines with no intention of returning? Why did I feel the need to prove that Filipinos can be as smart, driven, successful, and impactful as other ethnic groups in America? Why had I remained silent about harmful things I had seen and experienced? What took my power away, and how could I regain it back?

In order to complete this quest for understanding and leadership, I had to go to the Philippines after graduating from HKS. I had to wrestle with my cultural DNA and learn how the place where I came from affected my leadership style. I had to try. So, at the end of that year, I journeyed all the way to Manila, where I have lived and worked for the past four years.

I knew I had to go to the Philippines, but I boarded the plane unsure of how I would adapt to my new surroundings. No sooner had I landed in Ninoy Aquino International Airport that I found myself addressing others as "Miss" or "Sir" instead of calling everyone by their first name, as I usually did. I began to punctuate each "yes" or "no" with "po", a suffix in Tagalog added when addressing an elder or someone with more (perceived or actual) authority. These might seem like small changes, but they created a distance between me and my interlocutors, implying that they had more authority or power than

I did. I was a young woman used to working side by side with my bosses as we stuffed envelopes for health-advocacy campaigns—yet, all of a sudden, I was showing subservience to people I had just met.

On the best days, it made me feel good knowing that I was respecting the cultural norms of the Philippines. On worse days, it felt like a violation of my feminist, Western upbringing—why was I deferring to people simply because they were older, wiser, richer, or more established than I was? What had they done to deserve that reverence? To be honest, it's an adaptation that I still struggle with, almost four years later. I cry less now, but every now and then I still have experiences that make me throw up my hands in frustration and wonder if I've done the right thing in coming here, at the expense of friends, family, a more lucrative job, and other creature comforts available in the U.S.

The change in myself also made me think about other visitors to Asia. If I could be swayed by the power dynamics in the Philippines, one of the most Western of the Asian nations, how would people from other countries respond to them? How would I fare in countries like Korea, Japan, or China, where I would be teaching during this fellowship and where public perception and even popular culture suggests an even more rigid power structure? Given these circumstances, I didn't know how I could expect my students to tackle issues like what it means to work and live in Asia and how the constraints of tradition, a rigid social hierarchy, and unequal power dynamics affect individual actions.

Case-in-Point: Topia

I accepted my teaching fellowship with the vague notion that authority and power structures would play a critical role in my classes. The way my students responded to my authority as a teacher would give me lots of information on both their instincts about leading others and the constraints they felt from their societies, communities, and families.

Knowing that my students would be in high school and would come from widely varied backgrounds, I chose not to have them prepare individual case presentations. Instead, I decided to design a single case that we could cover as a class over the course of the five sessions. The case had to be interesting enough to keep the students engaged. Since I would be teaching students from South Korea, Japan, China, Kyrgyzstan, India, Vietnam, Malaysia, and the Philippines, I did not want to create a case that would invite the students to engage in nationalistic thinking, which might prevent them from coming up with creative solutions.

Where did this leave me? With aliens, of course.

I wrote a case with the title "Topia," in which the students had to ensure the survival of the human race. Their task was to find a way to recover from an alien invasion that has destroyed every part of the world except Asia. The aliens have left a wake of destruction similar to nuclear fallout, including a radioactive-like gas, which can be counteracted only by a plant, which could be found only on a remote island in the Pacific Ocean. As a class, the students had to figure out how to guarantee the survival—and eventual thriving—of the human race when most international legal structures have crumbled and a vast majority of the human population have died. In a nutshell, I wanted the students to think about what the future of Asia would look like if they could create it from scratch, with no influence from the rest of the world. Would they choose to stay within their current frame of reference, resorting to tribalism and fighting over natural resources, thus forming a dystopia? Or would they opt for a more creative, collaborative approach, thus forming a utopia?

*

I entered the first-floor classroom at the George Washington Incheon Global Campus prepared to provoke my students. After two days of intense lectures, I felt that the time had come to turn up the heat. At some point over the course of the night's lectures, I would sit down. Without giving notice or context—I wanted to see how the students would react when the authority in the room disappeared. Their responses would show me, through a case in point, how they were likely to approach the Topia case.

The night before, I had also sat down, but only after inviting two students (who had asked for permission to speak) to share their recommendations on the Topia case. They proposed an approach based on their experience as Model UN delegates. Their classmates sat and listened, but with my guidance—and with assistance from Craig Brimhall, another Teaching Fellow whom I had planted in the room—the class ultimately chose to stick to the status quo. They would approach the case as I had written it, in small groups and not as a Model UN case with each student representing a nation. In other words, they had given me the benefit of the doubt, assuming that there was some greater lesson in the way I had written the case.

That night, when I sat down, things felt different. At first, the students didn't know how to react. I waited unwaveringly, counting "one Mississippi, two Mississippi…" in my head as the silence in the room became more palpable. I had reached "three" when Enzo jumped out of his seat and ran toward the podium. Grabbing the microphone, he launched into what I suspected was a Model UN procedure, opening the floor for motions—presumably to reignite yesterday's debate and get consensus to change the case structure to suit his preference. Familiar with his way of doing things, Harry and Matt started to spar with Enzo. Suddenly, the class seemed to be located in the Philippines, where all three of these boys came from, instead of in South Korea, where we actually were, in a classroom with thirty-eight students from eight countries.

As if an alarm bell had gone off in his head, KJ—who the night before had argued that the class should follow the case as it was written—got up and said, "I make a motion to remove this chair from his position. Any seconds?"

A hand shot up. Then a series of other hands appeared. Finally, a "Second" hushed the room. I stood and approached the podium. Defeated but not deterred, Enzo stepped aside and went back to his chair.

This interlude lasted for about three minutes, but in that short amount of time the students had generated more conflict than even I had anticipated. It was time to organize the chaos. "Can anyone tell me what happened here?" I asked. I glanced around the room, surveying the class for some indication of where they stood. Students averted their gazes when I looked at them. They shuffled their weight from side to side. A couple of the more defiant ones looked at their cell phones, even though we had deemed the classroom a phone-free zone.

At last, sensing their reluctance to volunteer answers to such an open-ended question, I tried again. "How many students are there in this classroom?"

"Thirty-something?" came a sheepish reply from the back of the room.

"How many people have been speaking in the last three minutes?"

Murmurs of "Five," "Seven," "Boys," "Filipinos." Then silence.

Finally, a hand rose at a corner of the classroom that had been especially quiet. "Guys, we discussed this yesterday. Miss Ami gave us a structure and a mandate to discuss the case in small groups. We tried to debate it as a large group, but it's clear that we're incapable of doing that."

Akim had sent a volley. Would someone play this game with him?

As if catching a ball, Jimmy spoke. "We haven't heard from over thirty people in this classroom. We should give space for each person to talk. Why don't we see if we can make progress on the case in our small groups?"

I took their lead. "You've got a proposal on the floor. Who agrees to tackle this case in small groups?"

Thirty hands went up in the air.

"Okay. Let's spend the next fifteen minutes brainstorming options for the case in your small groups. When you've got some ideas to share with the class, I'd like the women, whom I have not heard from, to represent your small groups."

Immediately two hands shot up. "Miss Ami, we've been talking!" Alex and Sabrina felt unheard, and they were right.

*

Cambridge, Mass, September 2012. Ron Heifetz was at the front of the room, talking about the concept of "tuning." He is a cellist and often uses musical metaphors to explain what he taught. As a violinist, I related. Ron said that sometimes we hear something and it resonates so much with us that we feel the need to speak up about it.

I raised my hand. It was the first or second session of our Adaptive Leadership class, and only a few students have spoken. Ron invited me to speak. My palms started sweating, and I felt a lump in my throat. One hundred and forty pairs of eyes had turned in my direction, sending all sorts of messages: "Who is this girl, and why does she want to speak now?" "What could she possibly have to say?" A moment before, I felt compelled to speak, urged by some invisible force. Then, I wanted to crawl in a hole and die. But I would have to speak.

"Professor Heifetz, I was just wondering—in the time that you've been speaking and asking us to contribute, I've only heard from the men in the classroom. Why have none of my female classmates spoken up?"

With a twinkle in his eye, Ron sat down.

*

When Alex and Sabrina called me out and reminded me that some women had, in fact, been speaking, I could see the light-bulb go off in their eyes, just as it had for me when I raised my hand in Ron's class five years ago.

What happened next threw us all in a loop. As the young ladies who represented the small groups came up to brief their classmates, they created space for the other female students to speak. Every single women in the class spoke that day. Some had trouble expressing themselves in English, but their teammates—both men and women—encouraged them, patiently waiting for their thoughts to come out. Like a wave that went back to the ocean after a storm, the chaos of the previous ten minutes subsided, and a new tide came in.

I could see enthusiasm and discovery shining in those students' eyes. Regardless of gender, background, ethnicity, and nation, each of them left class that day with the knowledge that exercising leadership does not require you to be loud or brash. It could be done with a simple, quiet gesture, as long as that gesture brought others along with you.

From Padawan to Jedi (Spirit)

In the short span of those five days, my students had gone from being quiet and unsure of themselves to working together and solving a challenge in a new way. By the end of it all, they and I, were exhausted.

After class one day, Jimmy approached me. He hadn't spoken much in previous sessions, and yet tonight in our group discussion he had felt moved to speak. "Miss Ami, I have a question," he said now, clutching his notebook. "You said that leadership is something you have to practice, and that you are giving us the space to do that in this class. But I don't think my comments in class today made sense. I felt kind of..." He trailed off and shuffled his feet, his gaze shifting from side to side.

After a few seconds, I volunteered an adjective: "Strange?"

With a sigh, he said, "Yes." He made a motion toward his gut, as if he were stirring something inside.

Sensing that he was wrestling with this feeling, I said, "Your intervention in class today was successful. Why? Because you were able to guide your classmates toward a new course of action. You moved us away from chaos toward a productive discussion that generated meaning and helped us work on how to solve this case."

His shoulders relaxed, his backpack sat more comfortably on his back.

"And that feeling?" I went on. "I feel that every single time I walk in or out of the classroom. But conversations like this one are what motivate me to keep trying, even though it never goes away."

May the Force Be with You

Teaching the AULS students was one of the most challenging and rewarding experiences of my career as an educator. I hope that in giving my students the space to try new ways of doing and thinking, even if it made them uncomfortable, I've contributed to their education and development.

The Topia case was fictional, but the challenges my students are going to face are ones that, similarly, don't have a straightforward nature or one simple solution. What's more, they will have to figure out solutions for these challenges not just with other Asians but in an increasingly interconnected world. As I explained to the class at the end of our time together, everything I did in our workshops—whether improvised or planned—was done in the service of their learning. My wish for them—as it is for you—is that they can take something of what they've learned and put it into practice the next time they face a challenge or question. You might end up making the same decision as you would have made before reading this. Maybe, just maybe, you might find the mind, the heart, the gut, or the spirit to do things differently.

| Chapter 3 |
Teaching Adaptive Leadership in Kyrgyzstan:
Work in Practice and Reflections

Philipp Essl
MPA, Harvard Kennedy School of Government
Umar Shavurov
MPA, Harvard Kennedy School of Government
Hungsoo S. Kim
MPA, Harvard Kennedy School of Government

● ● ●

Introduction

It all started in the spring of 2012, over the course of a few meetings in Lamont Library at Harvard University. During these meetings, the three of us—Samuel Kim, Umar Shavurov, and Philipp Essl—discussed the idea of sharing the knowledge and inspiring insights we had gained from our studies at the Harvard Kennedy School (HKS) with an audience that was not able to access them directly.

Soon afterwards, Samuel, along with his colleagues from Harvard, started to build a thriving group of non-profit organizations, which today connect the vast educational resources of such world-renowned U.S. institutions as Harvard and Stanford with individuals and organizations in Asia, who are working to address the region's socioeconomic challenges of the 21st century[1]. It would take another five years until the three of us finally joined forces again, first on Skype, to collaborate on one of the subjects that had become most important to us during our time at the HKS: the practice of Adaptive Leadership, taught in one of the most highly acclaimed and sought-after courses at Harvard, a course voted by alumni as having made the biggest impact in their lives and careers[2].

Upon returning to his home country of Kyrgyzstan, at the end of 2016, after ten years abroad, Umar designed a two-day Adaptive Leadership program for September 2017 it was to be conducted in the country's capital, Bishkek, for seventy-two participants from the private, public, and NGO sectors.

Both the conceptual framework of Adaptive Leadership and the experiential methods of teaching and learning about it left us deeply intrigued and inspired during our studies at Harvard. The concept considers leadership as a practice or activity rather than as a certain role or set of characteristics. Leadership depends on what you do, not who you are or where you sit in the hierarchy of an organization. It is different from both authority itself and positions of formal authority. Holding an executive management role in a company doesn't make you a leader.

Distinguishing leadership from authority is empowering because one realizes that leadership is not a craft limited to a few chosen ones. It is a possibility and responsibility that we can all choose to act upon,

---

1 The Centre for Asia Leadership, http://asialeadership.org/.
2 As described in *Leadership Without Easy Answers* by Ronald Heifetz and taught at the Harvard Kennedy School by Professors Ronald Heifetz, Dean Williams, Hugh O'Doherty, Tim O'Brian, and Farayi Chipungu.

if we are committed to helping our communities and organizations thrive and to tackle the really tough problems that we can only confront collectively. Exercising adaptive leadership means mobilizing others to address a challenge[3] that cannot be solved with a technical fix by a single person or a group of experts. Instead, such challenges often require painful changes in behaviors, attitudes, and beliefs by many people who are part of the issue.

Consider the following case. A faulty heart might be fixed by a surgeon through an operation—a technical fix—if the underlying issue is a pathologically deficient chamber of the heart. But if the underlying problem was an unhealthy diet or a lack of exercise, the operation alone would not do the trick. A change in lifestyle—an adaptive solution—will be required for the patient to get better in the long run.

Distinguishing adaptive challenges from technical challenges and linking the practice of leadership to the former are important strategies because they help us direct our attention and focus on the tough issues that require collective problem-solving. It can be disenchanting and sobering to wrestle with the implications of not having ready-made solutions at one's disposal. Adaptive work requires experimentation, a stomach for uncertainty, ambiguity, and frictions, and the ability to keep oneself and others in the game during moments of despair and frustration.

---

3   Similar to what is often referred to as a "wicked problem," as described by John C. Camillus (2008) in "Strategy as a Wicked Problem," in *Harvard Business Review*.

The Purpose of This Essay

While the three of us have wrestled extensively with a range of adaptive challenges in our professional lives, we believe that elements of our Adaptive Leadership program in Bishkek illustrate some of the key challenges of exercising leadership. In our case, the leadership task was to mobilize a diverse group of workshop participants to learn about leadership in ways that contradicted their existing assumptions, beliefs, and expectations of what leadership is, how it ought to be taught, and how it should be practiced.

The primary purpose of this essay is to reflect upon our teaching experiences in Kyrgyzstan as an adaptive leadership challenge in itself. Our reflections focus on actual workshop dynamics that arose between participants and the teaching team, as well as on key distinctions and concepts of the Adaptive Leadership framework[4]. We do not intend in this essay to provide a comprehensive explanation of the Adaptive Leadership framework but rather to encourage the reader to think about leadership opportunities in everyday life, especially in the context of activities and tasks that we would not usually associate with leadership.

Preparing the Adaptive Leadership Program in Bishkek

Our workshop preparations began in the summer of 2016, when Samuel and Umar led a group of graduate students from Harvard, MIT, Tufts, and Columbia on a Trek through Central Asia and Kyr-

---

[4] For more information about the Adaptive Leadership framework, please refer to *Leadership Without Easy Answers* by Ronald Heifetz.

gyzstan was one of the four countries they visited. In their encounter with local thought-leaders and decision-makers, during which a wide range of socioeconomic challenges were discussed, we realized the important role that Adaptive Leadership could potentially play in addressing these issues. A few months later, Umar and his family moved back to Kyrgyzstan after close to a decade of overseas life, and Umar started to explore more concretely how to introduce Adaptive Leadership into his country of birth. In April 2017, Samuel, Umar, and Philipp agreed to conduct an introductory, two-day Adaptive Leadership workshop in Kyrgyzstan in September 2017. This was part of a broader strategy to support the development of "real" leaders in Asia from an Adaptive Leadership point of view[5].

Prior to the arrival of the team in Kyrgyzstan, we took two important actions that helped us to gain an initial understanding of the prevailing perceptions of leadership among both the broader public in Kyrgyzstan and our workshop participants specifically.

Firstly, Umar published an article in one of the local online newspapers, explaining in simple terms the main ideas behind Adaptive Leadership and promoting our workshop. The article invited readers to take part in an interactive survey to explore their mental models of leaders and leadership. The respondents had to associate their personal understanding of leaders with a predetermined list of multiple-choice options from the animal world: a lion, a gorilla, and an owl. The results—most respondents chose the lions, followed by the gorillas—provided valuable insights into the public perception of leadership in

---

[5] See Dean Williams (2005), Real Leadership: *Helping People and Organizations Face Their Toughest Challenges.*

Kyrgyzstan, and we subsequently used them during the workshop.

Secondly, we asked all the workshop participants to submit a brief essay on a personal leadership failure prior to the workshop. This was crucial in helping us to prepare for the workshop because it provided us with important insights into the participants' leadership challenges, in terms of their underlying assumptions, expectations, aspirations, and priorities. What stood out across these essays was a desire for the teaching team to provide quick and easy recipes for creating a following among people's constituencies, based on more conventional understandings of leadership.

Finally, on the ground in Bishkek, five days before the workshop, we closeted ourselves in Umar's apartment, enjoyed the delicious food and desserts of Umar's wife, Ann-Marie, and discussed the values, expectations, and goals that each of us was bringing to this exercise. We were united by the shared purpose of introducing Adaptive Leadership as a framework that would allow people in Kyrgyzstan to generate new diagnostic and action strategies, so that they could make progress in solving their most pressing problems.

Over the next five days, beginning on September 3, our design and preparation work touched upon the following elements and challenges.

Group Size and Diversity

Due to our marketing and pricing strategies, the team decided to allow open enrolment. We ended up with seventy-two participants. There were participants as young as fourteen and some older than fifty; 60% were women and 40% men; over a dozen ethnic groups were represented, including both citizens of Kyrgyzstan and other countries like Kazakhstan; there were people from the government, private, and non-profit sectors. In a way, we had gathered together a microcosm of society in Kyrgyzstan.

Although this diversity was pleasing in that it met our desire to replicate the real world inside the workshop auditorium, it created enormous challenges in designing the teaching program. In particular, we struggled to find the right set of cases to illustrate key concepts, given the diversity of the group. For instance, historical references to the Soviet Union and its authoritarian system might not resonate with the younger participants, who were born after the collapse of the USSR. Instead, we had to find cases that would be familiar to most of the participants, such as the pollution problem in Bishkek.

Workshop Content

We faced a dilemma in formulating the theoretical content of the workshop: a balance had to be struck between depth and breadth. Given the novelty of the Adaptive Leadership framework in Kyrgyzstan and the diverse professional backgrounds of the workshop participants, we limited the amount of framework components to allow for the participants' capacity to process and apply the workshops' concepts to their own leadership challenges in a meaningful way.

Workshop Methodology

Improvisation is one of key principles of Adaptive Leadership. Early on we agreed that, although there would be a teaching plan, improvisation and adaptation would be useful to ensure that we were "reading" the class. Sticking to a strict agenda might be useful in reaching the overall goal, but it might also come at the cost of losing some people simply because they couldn't understand the concepts. The most difficult part was agreeing on the right balance between conventional and experiential teaching methods. The former consisted of conventional presentations, facilitated group discussions, and small-group work, while the latter used group dynamics among participants and the teaching team to demonstrate key concepts in real time. In determining the right balance, we again considered the local cultural context and familiarity with traditional teaching methods, the participants' professional backgrounds, and the capabilities of the teaching team to productively manage complex group dynamics in real time so participants could learn from them.

Teaching a Team Dynamic

Two of the most important elements of Adaptive Leadership are the ability to distinguish between the *role* and the *self* and the ability to pause in the midst of action and *reflect*. We adopted these principles as guiding posts, agreeing that, if one of us noticed a behavior or pattern that would not be productive in reaching our goals, we would call that member out. We also agreed that when tense moments arose, we would pause and reflect on what was going on to see whether or not the discussion was helping us meet the broader goal.

Within any group there will be hidden issues, conflicting views, unresolved concerns, different factions and sub-factions, and competing needs and interests. As we discussed the overall approach of the workshop, we saw that our views were starting to diverge from each other. Umar strongly desired to conduct a workshop that would unsettle existing norms of leadership and shed a new light on the shared responsibility of the people of Kyrgyzstan with regard to the collective challenges faced by the country. Samuel held the perspective that the workshop should be pleasant and enriching for its participants, since the objective was to help the participants understand that leadership and its practice cannot be achieved overnight; for this reason, he felt that we should view the workshop as a way to plant the seed for future workshops and recurring participants. Philipp was of the opinion that we had to strike a balance between taking people out of their comfort zone and enticing them to want more of Adaptive Leadership.

Leadership Challenges in Delivering the Adaptive Leadership Program

Afterward, as we applied an Adaptive Leadership lens to our actual teaching experience, we were flooded by a seemingly endless stream of thoughts and insights. For the purposes of this essay, we will summarize four of these insights, which not only provide rich sources of learning about the challenges of exercising leadership but can also be easily related to and transferred to non-teaching leadership contexts.

The Importance of "Initial Events"

Adaptive Leadership, particularly as practiced at the HKS, hones students' awareness of a phenomenon referred to as the "initial event."

In many situations when people come together to pursue a certain work, whether it be a new working group in an organization, a new group of students, or simply a group of friends or neighbors, what happens in the first few moments of being together can have a formative impact on the dynamics and functioning of the group. A person might arrive late to the first meeting and subsequently contribute less to the discussion, due to a feeling of guilt. Another person might be the first to speak up and make a useful suggestion on how the group can work together, thereby gaining a special if informal status within the group, which in turn might influence the way his or her future suggestions are considered, compared with those of other colleagues.

In our workshop experience in Kyrgyzstan, part of our "initial event" was an opening exercise that we referred to as the "puppeteer exercise." The exercise consisted of the facilitator providing instructions, such as to "sit down," "stand up," or "turn around," and the participants complying with these instructions. The facilitator does not provide any explanation or clarification but simply states the orders. During the debrief after the exercise, another facilitator then discusses the exercise's purpose, which is to illustrate the concepts of *authority* and *power* and how they both differ from the notion of *leadership*. By conveying orders without a real purpose, one demonstrates how authority, and people's assumptions about it, can be misused; true leadership, in such a case, is lacking.

After extensive deliberation during our preparation work, we also agreed to use the exercise to push workshop participants out of their comfort zone. We wanted to signal from the very beginning that this leadership workshop would be different from others, both in its content and in its experiential approach to learning. Umar took on the role of the "person in the driver's seat," since we expected him, as a Kyrgyz national, to be the most influential in unsettling our workshop participants. Philipp was tasked with debriefing with the group and redirecting their attention to learning from the exercise.

During the workshop, however, we were taken aback by the emotional intensity of the exercise, compounded by Umar's authoritarian delivery of it, as well as a few unrelated logistical issues that had already upset several participants upon their arrival. One could feel the disappointment and anger in the group. Many of them knew Umar in person and felt betrayed. Philipp's efforts to help make sense of the educational insights of the exercise did little to change this. During our feedback session at the end of the workshop, one participant expressed her feeling toward Umar as "hate." She said that it had taken her until the second day of the workshop to recover from her initial negative emotions toward him.

This example demonstrates in a powerful way the significance that "initial events" can take on. The damage to what we had meant to be a safe learning space was done. We had incurred a significant loss in trust and rapport, from which, arguably, we never fully recovered.

The Importance of a "Holding Environment"

The Adaptive Leadership framework refers to the "holding environment" as the container that holds a group together, so that the group can do its work. We often illustrate the purpose of a holding environment by using the pressure-cooker analogy. A pressure cooker provides the "holding environment" required for the transformation of food ingredients into a finished meal. To turn pieces of vegetables into a vegetable soup, the cook needs to allow the pressure to build up, while at the same time regulating it so that the cooker doesn't blow up.

A similar phenomenon occurs in organizations, teams, and communities, and especially in learning environments, such as the one we created for our program in Kyrgyzstan. For people to open up, challenge, and even change their belief systems and habits, a certain degree of external pressure is required. In this case, to facilitate meaningful learning, the three of us needed to create a holding environment that would foster trust between participants and the teaching team and provide a safe space for people to share a wide range of perspectives. In this situation, a certain amount of tension is needed to shake up the system, but it should be contained within the group's holding environment, so that it doesn't impede the group's ability and desire to learn. Building and managing such a holding environment, using various tools—job descriptions, line-management structures, and explicit rules and procedures, but also a shared purpose, common values and traditions, trust, even physical spaces—is one of the primary tasks of a leadership team.

Reflecting upon our own workshop experience, we discussed the actions we had taken to create a holding environment that would facilitate the collective learning process. We intentionally used our Harvard background in the pre-workshop communication materials in order to establish our credibility and to instill trust in our ability to support people's learning about Adaptive Leadership. We also chose a venue with an open space that allowed for a conducive learning environment.

However, in retrospect, we failed to take several other actions that would have strengthened our holding environment. To start with, we could have organized a welcoming dinner on the night before the first day. This would have allowed for informal introductions and the building of trust among the workshop participants and the teaching team. It would also have allowed us to understand more fully the participants' expectations, stories, and priority issues, and to prepare accordingly.

We also underestimated the importance of setting the stage at the beginning of the program and elaborating on the assumptions, norms, and rules of the workshop, rather than just mentioning them. Allocating more time for an in-depth opening discussion would have signaled and reinforced our commitment to creating a safe place for people to open up, share, and experiment. We should also have explained in more detail why we had asked participants to submit a short write-up of a past leadership failure and reassured them that this information was being treated as strictly confidential. Simply sharing a leadership failure in itself can be a significant challenge in many cultures. By not acknowledging this, we missed the opportunity to build a holding environment that would be conducive to such sensitive conversations.

These lessons apply to leaders outside the classroom as well. Challenging people's values, beliefs, and behaviors in organizations or communities creates tension, conflict, and anxiety. To contain such frictions and keep people engaged in what is often painful adaptive work, without prematurely restoring the equilibrium, requires the fostering of a strong holding environment.

Using Authority Effectively When Exercising Leadership

Authority relationships and dynamics are hard-wired into people and organizations. Our dependence on authority starts from the moment we are born, when we look to our mothers for protection and direction. In the Adaptive Leadership context, we think of authority as a *de facto* service relationship[6]. A person is given authority by a group of people with the expectation that he or she will deliver a certain service to the group. We all know this dynamic from our own lives, when we expect our superiors and politicians to provide us with "the rights answers" or to release us from discomfort by solving an unpleasant problem on our behalf. The flipside of such a relationship is that we can take away the person's authority if we feel that our trust is betrayed and our expectations are not met. We can stop respecting and supporting our superiors, even if we still have to report to them, and we can stop voting for certain parties and politicians if we feel that they haven't delivered on their promises.

But what if our initial expectations are unrealistic? What if a problem can't simply be solved by the authority figure and instead requires the people themselves to adapt their beliefs and behaviors to a new status quo? In the context of our own experience, what if the workshop participants' understanding and expectations of our leadership and teaching methods were opposed to our new and unconventional ideas, concepts, and approaches to teaching and learning about Adaptive Leadership? This dilemma for people in formal authority positions is certainly one of the challenges we faced when we set out to

---

6   See Ronald Heifetz (1994), *Leadership Without Easy Answers*, p. 57

teach Adaptive Leadership in Bishkek.

One of our applied teaching methods, a "disengage exercise," illustrates a situation in which disappointing the expectations and potentially the trust of one's constituency might be required in the interest of furthering adaptive work—in our case, learning about Adaptive Leadership. The exercise requires the teaching team to disengage fully from any active classroom teaching or facilitation. While still physically present, we remained completely quiet for a total of forty-five minutes. The purpose of the exercise is to allow different forms of group and authority dynamics to emerge in real time—dynamics that can later be discussed and learned from. It was intended to be a powerful way for workshop participants to experience first-hand their dependency on authority and their inability to act and learn in its absence. At the same time, we hoped to witness the efforts of some workshop participants to exercise leadership and to start mobilizing the group toward its shared purpose of learning about Adaptive Leadership, through questions as well as more direct encouragement.

Despite our valid intentions for it, however, the exercise was poorly received, and several participants clearly felt disappointed in our failure to meet their expectations of having us teach in a more conventional way about leadership. Some even responded with anger, requesting that the authority figures return to the action and "do their job." At some point, the pressure was so high that threats of physical violence toward the teaching team were made, only half-jokingly. Various participants disengaged during this exercise, and a few even withdrew from the workshop altogether, not returning the next morning for the second day of the program.

This experience mirrors the real-world leadership challenge, faced by people in positions of formal authority, to "disappoint people's expectations at a rate that they can stand." One needs to retain people's authorization and trust in order to stay in the game, but at the same time one must challenge them enough to make sufficient progress against the real adaptive problem at hand. Doing so is easier said than done. It requires a strong holding environment and a process of trial and error, with multiple course-corrections along the way.

Taking Risks and Dealing with Failure

A process of trial and error lies at the core of tackling an adaptive challenge, since by definition there is no existing solution to the challenge yet. The same is true for the challenge of teaching, especially teaching Adaptive Leadership to a diverse group of seventy-two workshop participants in Kyrgyzstan. We believed—and still believe—that Adaptive Leadership is best taught in an experiential way, using the group and group dynamics as an opportunity for self-reflection and learning. Such an undertaking requires a stomach for uncertainty, ambiguity, and failure. For some of us, the last of these is the most challenging. We don't like failure; nobody does. But in a process of trial and error, failure is inevitable. It is simply part of the game that one needs to learn to play in order to be successful. In our case, failure arose partly because some participants did not return for the second day of the program, apparently considering that their time with us was not well spent. Viewing this proactively as a learning experience helped us not to get derailed. The feeling of having let people down is certainly hard to take in, but it comes with the territory of exercising leadership.

As important as embracing failure is the ability to receive criticism with grace and to learn from it rather than be paralyzed by it. Again, this is easier said than done. Some of the written feedback we received from the workshop participants who had left after the first day was personal and difficult to consider without letting our emotions get in the way. In such circumstances it is easy to become defensive, call a defeat, or simply get distracted by the tone of the message. Leadership requires the ability to listen carefully and learn from opposing perspectives and critical feedback, while at the same time holding steady in the face of undue criticism.

Concluding Remarks

We would like to end this essay with some final thoughts on the challenge and importance of developing Adaptive Leadership capacity at an organizational and societal level, as well as at the individual level, so that we can collectively tackle the most pressing adaptive challenges of our times: climate change, rising inequalities, forced migration, conflicts and diseases, technological disruptions, the digital divide, and bioengineering, among others.

To start with the country we taught in, Kyrgyzstan appears to mirror the broader developmental challenge that many countries in Central Asia are facing as they move from a Soviet mentality, a planned economy, and a societal top-down command structure toward a more dynamic and adaptive socioeconomic model, which is a better fit for a globalized world. While Kyrgyzstan stands out among its regional neighbors in its more liberal governance and economic model, it continues to face a range of significant adaptive challenges that will require its people to shift their values, norms, beliefs, and habits: corruption, poverty, unhealthy gender dynamics, the cultural dominance of the titular ethnic group, religious extremism, and more.

We believe that this transitional journey requires increased awareness of and reflection upon current authority relationship structures, the false dependencies they might create, and the ways in which they shape people's private and public lives. The limitations that traditional authority structures impose on socioeconomic innovation and progress need to be understood, and new models and ways of operating need to be designed and established. Building collective capacity in the practice of Adaptive Leadership—and in doing so bringing together people from all walks of life and society—would be a significant contribution to this undertaking. At the same time, it would provide a safe space for such innovation to take place.

On a personal level, the experience of teaching Adaptive Leadership is as rewarding as it is challenging and frustrating. In short, it mirrors the experience of exercising leadership in any other part of our professional and personal lives. It provides excitement and instills a sense of purpose, but it also, inevitably, leads to some failures and frustrations. One feels elevated and fulfilled when workshop participants reach new insights into themselves or leave empowered and inspired to make a real change in their communities and organizations, as we witnessed during our teaching engagement in Kyrgyzstan. But one might also experience despair and self-doubt, if the participants are not able to connect to the course material and class-room experience.

We believe that Adaptive Leadership can and must be taught—though this is a complex and difficult task. We experienced the challenge first-hand in Kyrgyzstan. How do you create an enabling environment that is conducive to the learning of seventy-two participants, when they significantly differ from each other in their private and professional backgrounds, as well as in their personal leadership journeys? How do you "pick people up where they are" and bring them along for a learning ride that will feel bumpy to different people at different times? How do you stay focused and committed in the midst of criticism and rejection, so that you can continue empowering people to become masters of their own lives? There are no easy answers or ready-made solutions to these difficult questions, but it is important to give it one's best try. The capacity to exercise Adaptive Leadership matters today more than ever.

Part 2

Asia Leadership Trek Essays

| Chapter 4 |

Onwards with Zeal and Zest:

An Engineer's Perspective on Continuous Leadership Learning

Puay Siang Tan

M.S., MIT School of Engineering & Sloan School of Management

• • •

The Asia Leadership Trek

"You are a trek maniac!" exclaimed a fellow Trekker during a meet-up two months after the Asia Leadership Trek Winter had ended. I had just asked when the next trek was. Being an engineer, having worked in the science and technology field for a decade (and still passionate about it!), I get excited about technical treks. As part of MIT's Master's program in Systems Design and Management (SDM), I have been to Japan and to San Francisco's Silicon Valley. These treks are focused on visiting tech companies and gaining an appreciation of how these companies drive innovations in their product designs and workplaces. I went on the ALT because it is a technical trek with a geopolitical flavor. It allowed us to explore challenges that various industries and organizations in seven Asian cities are dealing with at the socioeconomic and political levels. The experience provided me a different lens for looking at the impact of scientific and technological developments in society. Collectively, these treks have strengthened my belief in the importance of the continual promotion of science and technology to the younger generations and allowed me to peek into what makes an organization tick, thereby nudging me along the path of continuous leadership learning.

Science and Technology: The Gears that Drive Societal Growth

In these treks, the commonality that I observed is that science and technology play an integral part in promoting societal growth. Silicon Valley, home to big names like Google, Facebook, Apple, and Amazon, has developed exponentially due to the science and technology movement brought about by these tech companies. These tech giants have also brought along a set of peripheral businesses, including logistics and shipping, supply chain management, consumer products, etc. This development in turn has brought about job opportunities and an influx of people, which then drives further innovation and creativity.

Bangladesh and the Philippines, when we visited them on the ALT, seemed then to be on the other end of the spectrum. While countries like the US, Japan, and Singapore are riding the wave of the fourth Industrial Revolution and moving toward becoming smart nations, Bangladesh and the Philippines are struggling with telecommunications infrastructures and still striving to realize the benefits of the second and third Industrial Revolutions. Though the buzz that surrounds most of us now is how to enhance cybersecurity in the e-banking world, as the transfer of funds is made with several clicks and completed within minutes, on our Trek we heard of the two-hour commute by boat that people living in rural parts of the Philippines have to make in order to get to a bank!

Like a gear constantly moving (you can guess that my field is mechanical engineering), the forward movement of a country can be driven by developments and innovations in science and technology. For example, in countries where smartphone technology is a daily way of life, e-commerce has bloomed and people are continuously exposed to the frontiers of new technologies. On the Trek we visited the headquarters of a social enterprise in Japan called Digital Grid. The company provides low-cost, portable power sources to rural parts of Tanzania (areas not reachable by the national grid and hence almost without an electricity supply). We saw a mock-up store where people can rent and charge torchlights, which have a dual use as powerbanks. With light and portable electrical sources, the children in these communities can study at night, and the adults don't need to walk a couple of hours to the next charging point for their smart phones. While there is still a long "walk" ahead to the advent of technology for the members of these communities, their brightly lit homes provide both comfort and hope that they are on track to a better quality of life.

The Impact of Geopolitics

Motivated to explore the impact of geopolitics on the advancement of science and technology, I asked about it at least once in every country we went to on the ALT. I had an especially valuable chance to delve deeper into the socio-perspectives of this issue in Hong Kong.

The sight that greeted us at Hong Kong's Science Park was a "spaceship" structure that stood proudly in the middle of the campus. Extending from both ends of the "spaceship" were glass-clad link bridges joining two modern-looking buildings together. The Science Park is managed by the Hong Kong Science and Technology Parks Corporation (HKSTP), a statutory body set up to transform Hong Kong into a regional hub for innovation and technology development. I was excited as we walked through the "spaceship" toward our meeting with the CEO of HKSTP, Mr. Albert Wong Hak-Keung. Along the way, we saw a robotics center, incubation hubs, and many tech companies that had set up their offices there. In fact, the Park houses a total of 623 companies with a workforce of 12,000 people! Mr. Wong spoke passionately about Hong Kong's competitive edge and the initiatives that the HKSTP is driving, such as hackathons, incubation programs, and infrastructure support, such as laboratories and technical centers, to attract talents in science and technology into the compound. While it was a short meeting, I could feel a strong desire in HKSTP to elevate Hong Kong's global status in Science, Technology, Engineering, and Mathematics (STEM) through their active outreach to the world for collaborations.

It is important to explore how the education sector is driving science and technology development. One of the highlights for me on our trip was visiting the Hong Kong University of Science and Technology (HKUST). Personally, it felt like a homecoming, as I had done a one-month exchange in HKUST during my university days, forging lifelong friendships at its beautiful campus surrounded by hilly greenery on the beautiful Clear Water Bay Peninsula. We referred to this as "靠山面海" in Chinese, and it is one of the best "风

水" (i.e. good fortune). The red Sundial of the HKUST still stood prominently on the entrance patio, telling the time by the position of the sun. The sundial is one of man's earliest scientific inventions, and this red icon of HKUST, towering over us, seemed to be urging all its students and visitors to seize the day in pursuing their dreams. I snapped a couple of photos at the same spots where my friends and I had stood more than ten years ago and tagged them instantly on Facebook. Technology has sped up our pace; gone are the days when you had to wait days for photos to be developed from a roll of film (and only then realize you'd blinked!), and the name of the red Sundial— "Circle of Time" couldn't be more apt.

I kicked off our meeting with the Vice-President for Institutional Advancement, Dr. Eden Woon, asking him for his views on the development of science and technology in Hong Kong. Dr. Woon pointed out that Hong Kong was the first city to use a smart card— the Octopus Card—for train and bus transportation as well as payment for purchases at shops. However, it has lagged behind its neighbor, Shenzhen, China, in technological development over the past decade, since Shenzhen is home to multinational, high-tech, homegrown giants like Tencent and Huawei. Having an economy that is primarily focused on logistics, finance and tourism has further impeded Hong Kong's opportunities for technology development, a difficulty compounded by its minimal STEM ecosystem, which has led in part to the majority of the younger generation in Hong Kong not taking science and technology as their preferred major during tertiary education. The more Hong Kong is alienated from the STEM ecosystem and community, the harder it is for educators to attract students to this field.

While there is a respectable Science Park in Hong Kong, they have been struggling to retain the tech talent pool and to attract investments, since the opportunities are more abundant in Shenzhen. This has also led to the unwelcome cycle of students not being willing to take on a career in the science and technology field, as it would mean that they would need to work away from home for better job opportunities. Nevertheless, Dr. Wong told us about the relentless efforts by HKUST to groom the younger generations in STEM, forging collaborations with other institutions worldwide so that their students can gain exposure internationally. It is his wish that, in time, the city's perspectives toward science and technology will change for the better.

Having heard the views from the education sector and seeing for ourselves the infrastructure put in place in a bid to promote science and technology in Hong Kong, I reflected on how much effort the Government of Singapore (GOS) has placed in the social engineering field. In the earlier years of nation building in Singapore, there was a strong focus on the STEM fields as demands for manufacturing and production-related jobs were high. In the last fifteen years, the focus had shifted toward finance, as Singapore matured in her economy. However, that did not lessen the recognition of the need to maintain a talent pool for STEM, with the emergence of IoT, smart-cities initiatives, and cybersecurity threats (which can affect all sectors, beyond engineering and IT, especially the financial sector). The GOS over the last three years has strongly promoted STEM education so as to position its citizens for a new wave of technological and economic development.

The Importance of Education

When I saw my friend Kristine Soriano's Facebook post on her university graduation, as I headed back to Singapore, I became more convinced than ever that education is one of the most important enablers for leaders to bring their communities forward. Kristine was our local guide during the Philippines leg of the trek. Sitting in the same car, I noticed that she was constantly liaising with the contact person for the next place on our itinerary, ensuring that we would be on time, given the unpredictability of traffic conditions in Manila. Seeing Kristine's mega-watt smile as she wore her mortar board and convocation gown, I was reminded of the conversations we had on education in Manila.

We visited Enderun Colleges, an undergraduate college that offers degree and non-degree programs in International Hospitality Management, Business Administration, Entrepreneurship, and Economics. It is a beautiful campus, located in the financial district of Manila. The President of Enderun Colleges, Mr. Edgardo Rodriguez, shared his perspective on the key challenges that the Philippines need to grapple with, namely fighting corruption and complacency and changing the country's mindset. He felt that all educators have a responsibility to instill leadership in the youth and that it is important to "raise a new generation of wealth creators at home and not wealth seekers abroad."

As we conversed with Mr. Edgardo, I was inspired by his tenacity in wanting to make a difference in the Philippines. Through his own means as an empathetic leader, he is able to put himself in the shoes of those he is leading, and he is always actively learning and moving constantly. He was educated and taught in graduate schools in the

United States. Then he chose to return to Manila and work in the Asian Development Bank. After his retirement, he decided to manage Enderun Colleges. As this elderly gentleman escorted us around the college, I could sense his pride for his country and the sense of fulfillment that he gained from his work as the President of Enderun Colleges, whether he was engaging people and organizations that could contribute to the college's education roadmap or planting an idea in those he met to come together and help bring about forward development to Manila.

My guess is that although he could live comfortably overseas; it was the love for his country that prompted him to spend time building up the next generation of leaders in the Philippines. As he put it, the idea is "not to give up, start small—and, sometimes, that entails sacrifices." He does not see himself as having reached the "Age of Retirement" but rather the "Age of Fulfillment." He defines the "Age of Fulfillment" as a period when one is more liberal in taking risks, as he himself has demonstrated. To him, being in social entrepreneurship means that he can contribute back to society. As he stood by the entrance of Enderun Colleges, watching our vehicle drive off into the traffic, it felt as if our goodbyes were a path to a new beginning.

We also had the opportunity to dive deeper into the educational world and the development of science and technology from the perspective of the Filipino government, through interactions with Congressmen and a "Think Tank"—Stratbase Albert del Rosario Institute (ADRi), which is an independent research organization that primarily focuses on sociotechnical issues in the Philippines and East Asia.

In the current wave of technological development and innovations, ADRi feels that the Philippines have been only a recipient of innovations, and that more is needed to create an environment for innovation as well as promote an interest in science and technology in students, by making the subject interesting. I was elated to hear of the free college education that the Filipino government is pushing, as well as the newly set-up Science and Technology Departments in various universities.

Currently in the Philippines, schools are actually running in three shifts—meaning some classes are conducted at night!—due to the lack of facilities. While it may seem bizarre to have children sitting in classrooms at night, I could sense their hunger for knowledge and the pressing need for education. My hope is that as long as the government is cognizant of the situation and provides more access to higher and technical education to the people, coupled with social entrepreneurship movements, education for students in the Philippines will improve in the near future.

Leadership: The Engine that Makes an Organization Tick

In an ingrained, mechanical-engineer way, I have described science and technology as the gears that drive society forward, and that brings me to the next question: what drives these gears? To answer that we must look for the engine of the system.

The three treks I was involved allowed me to visit over fifty companies and organizations within six months in 2017. What struck me the most was the engine running quietly behind them. Many technological inventions and organizations are familiar to us in our day-to-day lives: the search toolbar that appears on everyone's internet explorer (Google), technological companies that put their products in almost every household (Huawei and Ericsson), the electric car that is taking the world by storm (Tesla), the traditional car-maker whose lean manufacturing is envied by all in the supply chain management (Toyota), e-commerce companies that fulfill your online orders in minutes (Amazon and Alibaba), train journeys that haven't been more than two minutes late in over a decade (Japan Railway), and non-profit organizations like the Red Cross, which is present in almost all disaster recoveries, to name a few. What is common in these organizations is that their people are motivated, driven, and charged up to perform. They have a personal stake in bringing their organizations to the next level. The leadership presence in these places, which I have likened to an engine, is what has driven these renowned organizations to their current successful status.

In some of the organizations we visited, we had the privilege of speaking with the CEO or top management of the companies and to hear their challenges and visions; in others, we met their engineers, domain experts, middle-level managers, and management trainees, hearing their perspectives and ideas for the company. In the following paragraphs, I will offer my observations on what the engine has done to make these organizations tick.

Let Your Guy Be the Boss!

One of the most significant leadership lessons I learned was from Mr. Matiul Islam Nowshad, the Chief Corporate and People Officer of Robi, the second largest mobile network operator in Bangladesh. When asked how he had motivated his staff and turned the company around to become successful, he revealed a human-resource management practice that he had developed. His employees are all encouraged to be entrepreneurs, and the company provides them with support and resources to found a startup. Every year, there is a competition within the company in which these budding entrepreneurs pitch their ideas. If selected, the company provides them with the funding and infrastructure to work on the project for twelve months, while still drawing their salary. If they are proven to be successful, Robi invests in these startups and the employee gets to own the company. If, after twelve months, the project does not work out, the employee goes back to his previous position. To me, this is a fail-safe creativity driver for all Robi staff who aspire to be bosses one day yet lack either funds to begin or needed job security.

So what is in it for Robi? Everything. Mr. Matiul mentioned that Robi prefers to work with companies that share the same corporate values, and the easiest approach is to have these companies led by their own staff, who understand Robi's values and work processes and will be in the best position to create value for Robi. The system reminds me of a Ted Talk by Dan Pink[1] on intrinsic motivators. Giving staff the autonomy to work on something they care about deeply instills in them a great sense of purpose and is an excellent driver for motivation. This is more powerful than extrinsic motivations, such as promotions or rewards. Our meeting with Mr. Matiul was like a breath of fresh air against the beautiful sunset we saw from Robi's conference room. Mr. Matiul invited us to partake in Iftar,[2] and I

---

1 https://www.ted.com/talks/dan_pink_on_motivation.
2 Iftar is one of the religious observances of Ramadan and is often done as a community, with people gathering to break their fast together. Iftar is taken right after Maghrib time, which is around sunset.

could feel his conviction, passion, and sincerity. He wants to empower his staff and make them their own bosses. This is a leader who has not failed to look back and help the next guy up the ladder.

Driving Toward Excellence

During MIT SDM's Tech Trek to Tesla in the Silicon Valley, I could feel the excitement emanating from the makers and engineers about pushing forward this innovative product. In the heat of the race for electric cars, these experts are stepping up to face the challenges in their respective domains: power trains, marketing, manufacturing, etc. It was immediately evident that Tesla is not just about Elon Musk or the other top guys. It is about what each employee can contribute to keep the company ahead of the race. A car is a complex system, and an electric car requires engineering that is different from that of a traditional gasoline car. To stay competitive, the various departments must function well with each other and work toward a common goal. In Tesla, the goal is to prove that an electric car can perform as well as a gasoline car. During our interactions with Tesla's staff, I could sense that each domain expert was empowered and had the drive to keep pushing boundaries and provide creative and innovative solutions.

Unifying Diverse Cultures

When we entered Alibaba's headquarters in Hangzhou, the big mascot and architectural design of the entire Alibaba campus gave us a sense of vibrancy. One could almost feel the pulse of the staff, each moving with purpose. We met with the management trainees under Alibaba's Academy program. This is Alibaba's special program for their foreign employees, in which they are put through a twelve-month program rotating through several departments, such as Sales and Finance, on a three-month basis. This is interlaced with a quarterly leadership program—one aspect of which involves trekking through the Gobi Desert with no means of communication! One of the guys we spoke to, Lereon, quipped, "There is no way my office could reach me!" What is powerful about this training program is its element of forced integration, which promotes an understanding of the cultural differences between the Chinese employees and the foreigners. One of the secrets to Alibaba's success: is its ability to gather talents from diverse backgrounds and cultures, encouraging them to work together and strive for value creation as all-rounders.

My reflections from the treks focused on the role of leadership in achieving organizational excellence. I believe everyone in an organization can exhibit leadership and contribute in a way that is valuable to the organization, and this concept brings me to the next segment I would like to present: learning how to be a good leader.

The Leadership Learning Journey: "Be Comfortable with Being Uncomfortable"

"Being Comfortable with Being Uncomfortable" was one of the most important principles of leadership that I shared with my workshop participants. They were mainly college and high-school students who attended the Asian Leadership Conference in the summer of 2017, organized by the ALT at Sunway University in Kuala Lumpur. As a facilitator of the workshop, I gained as much as (if not more than) the participants. I took a leap by testing a leadership model for achieving "Exceptional Leadership," which I had mooted during my classes at the MIT Sloan School of Management.

The experience was sometimes uncomfortable, as I was opening up myself to questions on my Leadership-Followership Model (see Diagram 1) rather than sharing well-defined methodologies and tools. Yet, after conducting the workshop with two different groups of students, I believe more strongly than ever that the more at ease we are with being uncomfortable, the more confident we will be to take on the next challenge.

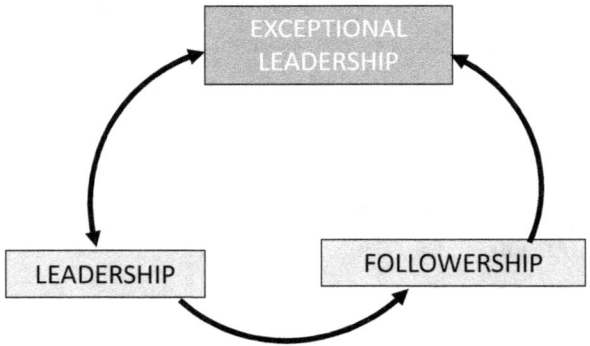

Diagram 1: Leadership-Followership Model

Leadership, Followership, and Exceptional Leadership are the three anchors in a continuous loop in this model. Followership is an interesting and infrequently discussed element in leadership. I believe that its meaning extends beyond the dictionary's definition of "following" or "capacity or willingness to follow." I see Followership as behavior that a good leader must acquire to become an exceptional leader. In a leadership role, if a person is also able to exhibit followership, he is placing himself in a continuous loop of improving himself, since he will be humble enough to learn from others (e.g. be a follower) and thus increase his competence and skill-sets so that he becomes more equipped to deal with new challenges.

My first realization of this Leadership-Followership model occurred with my classmates in my favorite class at MIT,[3] in which we staged *Macbeth*, a Shakespeare play, in front of two hundred people. In addition to being the actors (and each of us played at least two different roles), we also each took on a production role: stage manager, finance manager, director, music & sound technician, lights technician, makeup artist, props and costume manager, marketing manager. All of us had both a leader role and a follower role (e.g. the actors followed the director's leadership, and the director followed the guidance of the lights and sound technicians). While moving in this continuous loop, each of us learned something new and became better. As a director, I followed the lead of the lighting technician to create the right atmosphere on stage and learned a trick or two about controlling them.

In the following paragraphs, I will use the interactions in my workshop to contextualize the ideas behind my Leadership-Followership Model, breaking it down into five principles for learning to be a better leader. The workshop preparation began a day prior to the conference, when I met my teaching assistant, Mei Yen, a student at the Sunway University. I shared with her my workshop materials, research notes, and presentation slides. Then I tried to answer all her queries about the model, and we worked on how to fine-tune the workshop

---

[3] MIT Course No 15.282—Enacting Leadership, Shakespeare and Play.

to convey the concept of Followership effectively to the participants. I must say that the first thirty minutes of running through the slides was not comfortable, as I imagined thirty Mei Yens in the classroom the next day, questioning me and looking at me for an answer.

#1: An Exceptional Leader Must Know How to Be a Follower

There are times when others can and will lead better than you. This is the first part of the Leadership-Followership model, in which you "swing" from being the leader to being a follower. As leaders, we must constantly remind ourselves that the collective experience of all individual contributors in an organization is what makes you and the organization successful.

In my meeting with Mei Yen, I immediately recognized that she would be able to engage with the students more effectively, given the similarity in their experiences of working in teams in school, as compared with my own examples, which take place mainly at workplaces. I asked Mei Yen to be my co-facilitator, since I believed that she would be able to convey the idea better. Mei Yen did a great job explaining to the participants the five types of followers,[4] giving examples that she had encountered at school and that immediately struck a chord with the participants, opening up many discussion points.

---

4 The five types of followers are defined in Followership Model by Robert Kelley: The Sheep, The Yes-Person, The Pragmatic, The Alienated, The Star Follower.

#2: The Power of Teamwork

The achievements of an organization are the results of the combined efforts of each individual.
— *Vince Lombardi*

The power of teamwork is built upon our understanding that we cannot do everything by ourselves and that we need to be followers when others are experts in the subject at hand. We need to be agile in the model of Leadership-Followership, to "swing" from a leader role to a follower role. We need to recognize the person best able to take charge and exhibit the right competencies of a follower.

Working as a team in the Macbeth production, we needed to respect each other and follow each other's lead. What would have happened if directors had tried to take over the marketing job? While we could do our own "marketing" in convincing our friends to watch the play, it was better for us directors not to meddle with the agreed publicity strategy. Similarly, in props management, while the directors sometimes requested particular props, they had to be followers to the props team, lending support by simply giving instructions instead of getting involved in the procurement or purchasing. The negative effects, had we not followed this procedure, would have been threefold—the props team would have felt slighted, the finance manager might have confused the payment structures, and the directors might have become burnt out trying to manage everything else on top their own responsibilities. It was obvious that we all had to work together as a team.

I believe that the power of "teamwork" was a positive experience for us during the workshop. Mei Yen was able to jump in and out of the session strategically, bolstering my points, and we were able to adequately address the questions raised about the Leadership-Followership model.

#3: Followership at Its Best

As followers, we must be mindful not to become negative people by shooting down the ideas of others. In fact, if we continue to exhibit the traits of a leader—thinking independently, having the courage to stand up for what is right, and evaluating decisions and actions before following—we will fall into the category of "Star Followers."

Mei Yen effectively exhibited the traits of a Star Follower when she sought a clear understanding of my intent and what I wanted to deliver for the workshop. We felt a sense of fulfillment as we achieved the outcomes we desired, facilitating an experiential workshop in which participants found their own definitions for leadership through our exchange on leadership principles and followership concepts.

#4: Followership to Exceptional Leadership

When we find ourselves in our own domains of expertise, then we should lead shamelessly—a good word that I like to use in this context, encouraging both myself and others. Mei Yen, within our short first meeting, clarified the objectives of the workshop and prepared herself throughout the night with the additional materials I had provided. She was then able to co-facilitate confidently at the workshop, guiding participants who were either her age or older. Mei Yen gained valuable experience by facilitating a workshop (the first time for her!), and this no doubt has added to her skills in presentation and persuasion techniques. She offers a perfect example of cycling through the Leadership-Followership model in order to become an exceptional leader.

#5: An Exceptional Leader Makes It Easy for the Followers

Consider leading a sled-dog team: your role as a leader is not just to lead your team to your destination; you must also consistently look back at those following you. You need to make sure that everyone is keeping pace with each other and utilizing each other's abilities, so that the team of sled dogs can reach the destination in the shortest time possible. This was the advice of Mr. John Chambers, Executive Chairman of Cisco Systems, with whom I had a short conversation when he came to MIT campus as a speaker for a leadership seminar. His words stuck in my mind as a key to exceptional leadership. You need to make it easy for your followers to come with you, and to do so you should always look over your shoulder to see how they are doing.

I concluded my workshop with a set of 3Rs, explaining them as my wish for the participants after they gained an appreciation of the Leadership-Followership Model: I advised them to Read to know more, Reflect to capture what they had learned, and Redefine their own leadership paths. It was delightful when the participants reached out to me after the workshop to share what they had learned and express their appreciation for the ALT Trekkers.

The conference as a whole emphasized that education is a lifelong pursuit. The ALT Trekkers mostly had some working experience and are currently returning to academia to pursue more knowledge. Most of the participants were young aspiring students or teachers at the university who were interested to know what this gang of Harvard, Tufts, and MIT students would share with their students. The spirit of learning is not limited by our age or our stage of life. What is important is that we continue our learning journey, develop our own insights (and models!), and share with others what we have gained. The key is to be curious and humble, and to learn, as a follower, from everyone we meet along the way.

As I reflected on my learning journey during the treks, a spiral image, something similar to the spiral approach for project management (my work area) kept popping up in my mind. To crystallize what I had learned from the ALT, I created a "Spiral Growth Path," synthesizing the generous advice and ideas we had gained from all the leaders we met.

A Spiral Growth Path

There are six elements in this Spiral Growth Path (see Diagram 2): "Listen with Empathy," "Work on Your Quotient Index," "Have Mentors," "Get Feedback," "Celebrate Failures," and "Be Authentic." I have used this path to remind myself about leadership development.

The motion in the Spiral is not unilateral in direction; there will be times when we need to move back and forth on the spiral as we move along the leadership journey. In addition, the spiral does not stop with six elements: its spiral nature allows us to continue to grow as we learn. Different people might come up with different elements and different sequences as they move along the spiral. In the following paragraphs, I will share my thoughts on these elements in the sequence I have placed them.

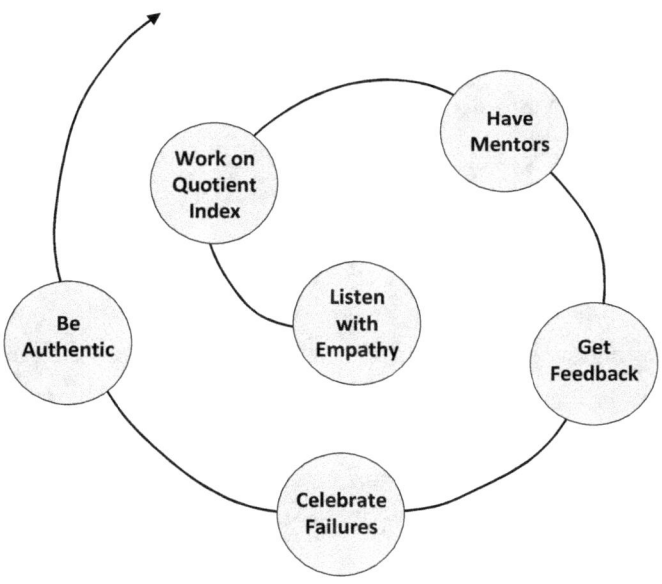

Diagram 2: Spiral Growth Path for Leadership Development

We need to begin with wanting to understand others better. To do that, listening is important, and listening with empathy is even more important. We may not have gone through the experiences that someone is recounting to us, but we can still "Listen with Empathy" and feel for ourselves the pain, joy, pride, discomfort, and motivation that the other person has experienced. These emotions are often unspoken, and we need empathy to hear what is not said.

"Work on Your Quotient Index"—what quotients, you might ask. The answer is for each one of us to define. The common quotients are the Intelligence Quotient (intellectual scoring), the Emotional Quotient (empathy and emotional-control scoring), and the Adversity Quotient (scoring to determine the ability to deal with adversity). As Mr. Lee Lung Nien, CEO of Citibank Malaysia, shared with us, the Likeability Quotient (LQ) and the Digital Quotient (DQ) are two new indexes that are also important, in terms of getting things done and enhancing effective communications.

LQ is about how others perceive you and "like" you. The higher the LQ index, the easier it will be to get assistance, thus increasing your chance of getting things done. LQ may also play a role in achieving the most favorable outcome in a negotiation, if the other party "likes" you. Many people whom I met on the Trek made me feel immediately comfortable and at ease with their approachable demeanor. In Chinese, we call this "人缘" (Rén Yuán). It is easy to see that the more you are able to "Listen with Empathy," the easier it will be to raise your LQ index.

DQ determines how well you communicate with others—customers, subordinates, bosses—through various social media platforms. The higher your DQ index is, the more effectively you will be able to communicate in our digitally enhanced world.

"Have Mentors" is like having an additional team member. It is important for us to have someone to talk to when we need advice, someone who can point us in the right direction or gently push open doors for us. We must be open to seeking out mentors (even if they are younger than we are!), because having mentors in all the different areas and aspects of our lives will help us to learn better. The higher our Quotient Indexes, the easier it will be for us to find mentors in the people we meet.

"Get Feedback"—one has to be comfortable in getting feedback and to be bold in asking for it. As everyone knows, getting feedback can be a stressful process. Remember your last feedback session with your bosses or someone important to you? We might feel encouraged if the feedback is positive, but, conversely, if the feedback is less than positive, we might feel discouraged, demoralized, or even defensive. However, it is important to listen to the feedback objectively and to reflect on possible development opportunities, so that we can improve our skills and continue to excel in areas where we thrive.

As a responsible leader, it is imperative that we work on our skills in giving and receiving feedback. The Growth Spiral then moves back and forth, covering and recovering the elements of "Listen with Empathy," "Work on Your Quotient Indexes," and "Have Mentors," which together form reinforcing loops with the element of "Get Feedback."

As we move along the spiral, we must adopt a willingness to "Celebrate Failure." Not only we should not be afraid of failures, we should feel even proud that we had tried and failed. Look upon your failures as achievements because they demonstrate that you dared to do something new, something different, something risky. When you are able to truly celebrate your failures, you know that you have taken bold steps out of your comfort zone and expanded the possibilities available to you. In fact, failures present great learning opportunities, allowing us to avoid future mistakes—so do not let those chances go to waste!

I have placed "Be Authentic" at the top of the upward spiral of the Leadership Growth Path, because "authenticity" in leaders is something that cannot be faked. As a leader, you must truly believe in what you are doing; this is what will make people to want to follow you. You must have the ability to weather the consequences of your actions, whatever they may be. For example, you may need to "Celebrate Failures" or "Get Feedback," looping back to the earlier elements of the Spiral to find more strength and resilience so that you can push forward toward what you believe in and ultimately carry it to fruition.

The mathematical equation for a spiral is a continuous one, and so is this Spiral Growth Path.

Onwards with Zeal and Zest

Onwards with Zeal and Zest, Forward We of CGS.
— Crescent Girls School[5]

The familiar tune and lyrics of my alma mater's song rang in my mind as I asked myself, "What will I take away from the ALT?" We had visited the sectors of education, finance, and technology in various countries; we had visited non-profit organizations and met political leaders. We had heard about successes, struggles, and challenges—but there was a common thread running throughout: everyone we met was charging forward with zeal and zest, because they knew the

---

5   Crescent Girls School. This is a secondary school in Singapore. The full lyrics of the school song can be found here: https://www.crescent.edu.sg/about-cgs/school-song-n-crest.

purpose of what they are doing. As I write, they are making a difference in the lives of others, and this is what makes their work meaningful.

This trek reaffirmed my conviction that the leadership path is constantly evolving. Leadership is not about having a pre-defined toolbox, from which you can easily pull out various methods of dealing with things or people; on the contrary, everyone needs to define and constantly refine his/her own leadership journey.

I would like to sum up with this quote from Mr. Lee Kuan Yew, the founding father of my home country, Singapore: "I do not know yet of a man who became a leader as a result of having undergone a leadership course." I have a lot of respect for Mr. Lee, for he has played a crucial role in bringing Singapore up from a small fishing village to the cosmopolitan city it is today. He has also played a big role in guiding future generations of leaders, keeping Singapore agile amidst an ever-changing world circumstances. As for my own take on leadership, I believe that advancement in science and technology is the key driver in bringing our communities forward. Education must be a relentless pursuit for all. Leadership must be a continuous learning journey. Let us all continue to be motivated to learn new things and lead in our own ways, so that all of us can contribute to our society.

Let your spiral grow!

| Chapter 5 |
Disrupt Yourself and Your Business Before You Get Disrupted

Jennifer Hurford
MBA/MPP, Harvard Business School

● ● ●

Introduction

My father always told me that thirty years of your life are for learning, thirty are for making a career, and thirty are for giving back to your institutions and community. Tragically, my dad's last thirty years were cut short: he passed away unexpectedly when I was in high school. So, I took on the mission of his last thirty—to make a difference in the world. When it came time to consider graduate school, I knew I wanted to find a way both to make money and to make a difference in the world—the two don't have to be mutually exclusive!

As a Vice President at Citigroup, I had completed a rotation program across Europe, the Middle East, and Africa. At the beginning of my career, I worked in London, Frankfurt, Cairo and New York, spending two years in each city where I had a chance to work with non-profit and impact investing outfits along the way. Given my varied and ambitious path, the Harvard Business School (HBS) and Harvard Kennedy School (HKS)'s joint degree program was the perfect match for my aspirations. However, I discovered after graduation that putting the theories I learned in practice was hard work – the theories on how to establish, grow, and run successful businesses need to be put into practice. This is the reason why I joined the Asia Leadership Trek as I realized theories could only take me so far.

It's one thing when you're in a classroom discussing with ninety other students what a CEO should do, while knowing that you'll be debriefed in an hour and find out exactly what he did do. It's another thing when you're sitting directly across from a CEO who is grappling with a strategic question about his business in real time.

During my three years in the HBS/HKS program, we read over six hundred cases covering a vast range of topics—from leadership, marketing, negotiations, and operations to finance and the global economy. We explored both the big and the small questions facing leaders in the government, private, and non-profit sectors. How do you motivate teams when your business is in decline and you need to cut costs to stay afloat? As a start-up expands, how do you ensure that the business's culture remains hungry and nimble and doesn't turn bureaucratic, stifling innovation? As a government official, how do you do what is right for your community in preparing for climate change, making investments to prepare for natural disasters and yet still connect with those who disagree with climate change and make sure you get elected in the next cycle? As an NGO founder, what is the right trade-off between using the funds that you raised toward the cause and using them toward overhead and hiring more people? As Chief Investment Officer for a wealth manager, how do you balance your fiduciary responsibility toward your clients with your responsibility toward your shareholders?

In educational programs, case studies offer simulations of such scenarios and challenges in order to prepare students for the time when they are in leadership positions and need to make tough decisions that will impact the lives of many. However, while learning from past situations can be helpful and informative, it is no replacement for hands-on learning in the real world. Business-school students have the benefit of hindsight and the resources of distilled lessons from dozens of cases, but when you are really in a leadership position and must make decisions with little or no time, the weight of the outcome rests on your shoulders and it can be an intensively stressful scenario.

As Asia Leadership Trekkers, we had the pleasure of meeting many leaders in the midst of making tough decisions. The following narration highlights two of the most important lessons we learned from them: (1) Disrupt yourself before you get disrupted—or self-innovation; and (2) If you don't take people with you on the journey, they'll reject the destination—or collaboration. These complementary lessons arose from our application of what we had learned in our business and public-policy schools to real-time leadership questions. In China, Bangladesh, Malaysia, and Singapore, we met with executives from a variety of industries: footwear, telecommunications, politics, and banking. All of these leaders helped us to understand and fully appreciate the importance of both self-innovation and collaboration with others.

LESSON 1: SELF-INNOVATION

Disrupt yourself before you get disrupted, in both business and the personal realm.

Case A: How to Grow in a Highly Competitive Market—Nike in China

Summary: *Nike, with its competitor Adidas on its heels, has counterintuitively decided to scale back the speed at which it opens new stores in China. Instead, it is innovating by changing its business model, adopting a digital-partnership strategy for customer acquisition, leveraging big data to inform and speed up its supply chain, and investing in robotics to innovate manufacturing.*

Traditionally, popular western brands have grown in China by opening new stores as fast as possible in all the cities with sufficient disposable income to meet demand. Operating stores means increased control over how potential consumers experience your brand, but it also means billions of dollars invested in fixed-cost brick-and-mortar retail, which is hard to swallow when demand doesn't pick up as expected in some cities.

China is a mono brand market, which means that Nike shoes are sold solely from Nike stores rather than from third-party retailers. However, Nike has discovered that increasing the number of new stores is a losing proposition, which is why the company has scaled back the number of its stores to 6,000 from 15,000. By contrast, and at the same time, Adidas increased the number of its stores in China by 20%.

Nike owns only 300 of its stores and relies on partnerships to operate the remaining stores. This is a risky strategy, as our Nike host, CFO of Nike China, Gavin Lindberg, recognized, because it entails relying on someone else to convey the Nike brand's look and feel. Retail-store concepts and distribution strategies can also be copied by competitors, who can simply walk into a store and snap pictures of in-store displays, shoe designs, purchase experience, and customer selections, later using that data to create their own retail experiences. In other words, what Nike gains by investing millions in design, customer-experience prototypes, etc., competitors can get for free.

For this reason, Nike has decided to disrupt itself before it gets disrupted by its competitors. Its leaders are now focusing on innovation in three areas in which they believe they can build a protective moat, as Warren Buffet says, making it harder for competitors to replicate their model: the digital arena, their supply chain, and manufacturing. By disrupting their current business model, they are foregoing potential short-term gains, but in exchange they are seeking greater rewards in the long term.

What will it take for Nike to win in the digital arena? I was amazed to see the expressions of revelation in the veteran executives' eyes as they recounted their shifting perspectives on selling their brand digitally. Three years ago, they resisted the idea of going on Tmall, Alibaba's business-to-consumer online retail platform. Two years ago, they agreed to go on it but believed that their own site, www.nike.com, would still lead. Today, they realize that it is imperative to be on Tmall. Though creating a digital solution for each market is expensive, Nike's leaders have come to realize that their digital solution for China must be market-specific and involve partners such as WeChat

(Tencent's social-media mobile application) and Tmall. "We can scale our own P&L, or we can leverage the ecosystem. We will need to leverage the ecosystem if we want to win in digital," they acknowledged.

There are over 900 million people on WeChat, and the average person checks WeChat 75 times per day. Increasingly, the common stance among consumers is that if they can't use WePay, then they are not interested in the brand. China's ecosystem is closed, and thus businesses need to be on that one app. In order for Nike to win in China, it has to win over the 450 million Chinese millennials—they are the most important consumer segment in the history of the world and it must be done through partnership. Nike's leaders have realized that they can't go it alone, and they have responded to this fact with innovation in their system, by finding retail-store operating partners and going on Tmall. Understandably, they want to control their brand as much as possible, but they know that partnership is the only way to grow in China.

What will it take for Nike to win with their supply chain? Nike has plans to develop a competitive advantage in its supply chain, something that Adidas and other competitors won't be able to replicate easily. The goals are to reduce the time to market from six months to two months, and to increase their responsiveness to their customers in order to incorporate fashion trends into their designs. The company will rely on big data to aid innovation in both of these areas, both to inform design and to help speed up the time to market.

What will it take for Nike to win in manufacturing innovation? Nike was one of the first brands to manufacture in China in the 1980s, and they benefited from the cheap labor prices. Today, however, they recognize that as labor prices rise, they can't chase cheap labor around the world anymore. But what if they took labor out of the product cycle entirely? Currently, over 250 people are involved in the production of a single shoe; what if that number was zero? What if knitting machines and robots did all the work? Imagine if you could have a shoe custom-made in Manhattan in two hours. That is the world that Nike is working towards, and its leaders believe that innovation along these lines will help them leapfrog over their competitors.

What does innovation theory tell us about whether or not Nike will be successful? When our meeting with Nike's leaders finished and we hopped back into the bus, I couldn't help but wonder what the future holds for Nike. Will they be successful in pulling off the new growth that innovation can bring? HBS Professor Clayton Christensen, famous for his theories of "disruptive innovation," says that it's difficult for most companies to succeed with innovation because "they don't understand their current business model well enough to know if it would suit a new opportunity or hinder it, and they don't know how to build a new model when they need it." Surely, Nike's leaders know their model well enough and know what they're doing in slowing the growth of retail locations in China, even if it means that Adidas will surpass them in brick-and-mortar locations and that their shareholders will question that choice. On the other hand, do they really need a new business model now? Are they switching strategies too soon?

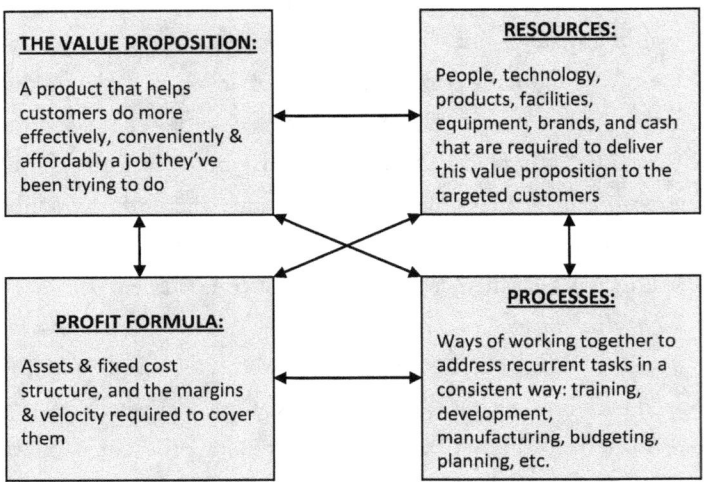

Source: Professor Clayton Christensen and HBS Coursework Diagram for "Building and Sustaining a Successful Enterprise"

Most successful companies operate according to a standard business model that can be broken down into four elements: a *customer value proposition* that fulfills an important job for the customer in a better way than competitors' offerings do; *a profit formula* that lays out how the company will make money by delivering the value proposition; and the key *resources* and *key processes* that deliver that proposition to customers. A new model is often needed, however, to leverage a new technology, or when a company must address an entirely new group of customers, or when a company needs to fend off a successful disruptor. Negligence or failure in business-model innovation is the primary reason why the leading incumbent firms in most industries typically fail when confronted by disruptive attackers[1].

One thing is certain, according to Professor Christensen's theory. Nike needs to make sure that the capital it invests in its business transformation is patient for growth and impatient for profits. More important than scaling the business is scaling the business profitably. "When a business scales its operations, it typically scales both the good and the bad, and as such, capital that is patient for growth has more time to figure out the inefficiencies in its business model before scaling. Capital that is impatient for profits tries to figure out a business' profit formula as fast as possible so that it can scale both the business and the profits[2]." Nike needs to make sure that it gives these new investments in robotics for the supply chain and manufacturing time to ramp up and grow, while at the same time they need to find efficiencies and profit opportunities so that the investments can start positively affecting shareholder value.

Only time will tell if the changes Nike is making today will enable it to win in China over the next decades. But its instinct for self-innovation is sound. The world is moving toward micro-segments of one—where once we used billboards to advertise to 80,000 people, we now use 80,000 different digital advertisements tailored to individuals. We live in a world where curation and customization are expected. Nike is betting that we will want the same in our shoes, and I think they're on to something by embracing innovation within their own company to meet the changing times.

---

1 https://hbr.org/2008/12/reinventing-your-business-model.
2 https://www.christenseninstitute.org/blog/eight-attributes-of-successful-market-creating-innovations/.

Case B: How to Change Your Company's Culture and Innovate Internally—Robi of Bangladesh

Summary: *Robi is the second largest Bangladeshi telecom operator. It offers pre-paid and post-paid mobile services, as well as value-added products and services such as mobile banking, fixed broadband, and international roaming. While the company dates back to 1997, Robi's name was born in 2016, when Axiata Group, Malaysia's largest mobile operator by market value, and Bharti Airtel, India's largest telecom operator by subscribers, agreed to merge their subsidiaries in Bangladesh[3]. "Robi" means "sun," representing the fact that the company aims to align its services with local Bangladeshi heritage and culture.*

The Bangladeshi telecom sector has experienced high growth and fierce competition among six major players over the last few decades. The merger of Axiata Group and Bharti Airtel to create Robi was designed to strengthen the industry structure and bring greater benefits to customers in terms of network coverage. The executive team we met on the Trek, however, recognized that the series of mergers had taken a toll on the company's culture and ability to innovate. They needed a new strategy to get themselves back on the map, so they created an in-house innovation arm to crowd-source disruptive idea from the employees closest to the customers.

Professor Christensen says that "over the long term, the greatest innovation risk a company can take is to decide not to create new

---

3 https://sg.finance.yahoo.com/news/malaysias-axiata-indias-bharti-merge-115709908.html.

businesses that decouple the company's future from that of its current business units[4]." Robi took that risk when it created an employee-only in-house innovation arm called "r-ventures." In recent years, the company has undergone a tremendous turn-around success story. The cost of doing business as a telecom company in Bangladesh is high, as the government has imposed burdensome taxes on the telecom industry, in contrast with textile companies, which get all the favors. Robi's leaders needed to find a way to inject the company with a fresh culture that would inspire employees to turn the company around from the inside. They did so using three valuable rules:

1. Operate with startup principles, even if you aren't one. Create opportunities for corporate intrapreneurship. R-ventures is an in-house incubator, a lean startup training program with over 200 participants. Ideas are pitched, and 10% are selected to be worked on by diverse teams across the firm. Employees stay on payroll for the year that they work on the venture. Robi then introduces the startups to venture capitalists and bankers, but it maintains the right to get first rights to equity investment.

2. When big changes are needed, empower a small team to make decisions quickly. Robi rapidly tested several organizational changes. As part of the company's transformation, the management team adopted a reward-driven culture: everyone is paid for the quality of their performance, which is measured by universal key performance indicators (KPIs) aligned with the company's revenue targets. Even an employee who serves coffee and Iftar, the Ramadan dinner, has KPIs that tie

---

4 https://hbr.org/product/the-hard-truth-about-business-model-innovation/SMR573-PDF-ENG.

back to revenue targets—he needs to make sure that he purchases food at an affordable price to feed all employees.

The company's leaders believe that incentive, performance, and engagement are all linked. They knew that if they wanted to improve the faltering morale of the company they would have to promote engagement, and so they created an open platform for employees to suggest changes. A management team of five read the suggestions and immediately sent out memos outlining the changes they had decided to adopt, making the employees feel heard and valued in a way that hadn't happened before.

3. *Culture eats strategy for breakfast.* It doesn't matter how good the corporate strategy is if the company's culture isn't strong and supportive. Robi discovered this, and it's leaders have been able to transform their company as a result. Not only is it back at the top of the telecom industry, it has been voted one of the best companies to work for in Bangladesh. Where once they were struggling to retain talent and market shares, today they are a success story that other corporations strive to emulate. They were able to disrupt themselves—to embrace self-innovation—and thus turn around their business in the face of extreme competition and government push-back.

Case C: Lessons on Life and Business—Our Interview with the CEO of Citibank Malaysia

Summary: *Your success is not defined by how smart you are. Play nice in the sandbox. In Malaysia we met with the CEO of Citibank Malaysia, Mr. Lung Nien Lee, who provided us with his insights on what it takes to have a successful life as well as a successful career. Today, more than ever* *given the competition for talent and the democratization of information, we need to build resilience and grit that will carry us forward on our life's journey toward personal and professional fulfillment.*

The CEO made it clear that to be successful in life, you need to develop more than just your Intellectual Quotient (IQ). You also need to strengthen your Adversity Quotient (AQ), Likeability Quotient (LQ), Diversity Quotient (DQ), and Emotional Quotient (EQ), in order to stay ahead and continuously work toward developing a better version of yourself. These are the insights he shared for these four crucial areas:

Adversity Quotient (AQ): The CEO explained that we must learn to take in other people's points of view, to receive criticism well, and to cultivate grit. Don't take the negative things that happen to you personally. Your choices are half chance, as are everyone else's.

Likeability Quotient (LQ): If people don't like you, then, no matter how smart you are, they will not help you. And this is where a lesson from kindergarten comes in handy: play nice! On some level the inner child is active even in adults. We are more likely to want to work with people for whom we feel a positive affinity.

Diversity Quotient (DQ): Don't surround yourself with people who look like you. It might feel good, but the market won't accept your answer. Companies should create teams that bring a diversity of perspectives. This diversity is critical because employees with varied backgrounds bring varied viewpoints that mirror the outside world. Diverse perspectives are necessary for creating meaningful work that will resonate with your consumer base. And your customers will reward you for understanding them by giving you their business. When it comes to creating customer-facing experiences, companies should have healthy debates in-house, rather than allowing their brand to be publicly tarnished with a poor and overly hasty decision.

Emotional Quotient (EQ): Connect with your audience using the tools they use. The CEO recounted a story about one of his main goals in life: to beat his fourteen-year-old son at FIFA on the Microsoft Xbox. The only way he can connect with his son is by doing the things his son loves to do, and for this reason he has embraced video gaming. We all need to develop the empathy required to understand different perspectives and adapt to what other people need.

In all of these areas, striving for change within ourselves will help us to interact more effectively with others. And as we have seen, the advantages of self-innovation are present for companies as well as for individuals.

LESSON 2: COLLABORATION

If you don't take people with you on the journey, they'll reject the destination. Develop a customer-focused mindset, when you're a government or a company.

Case D: Develop a Customer-First Business Strategy—Nike

Summary: *Senior management should keep a close eye on what the customer wants. Don't design what you want your company to put out in the world; instead solve a problem for your customers. This outlook is sometimes called human-centered design. When it comes to China, Nike believed that they need to adopt a China-first approach.*

Nike's customer-oriented approach in China appears in their product development, in their shoe design, and in their marketing. Instead of waiting for teams in Oregon to make decisions on what's cool in China, the local team relies on information from local consumers when making their decisions. For example, when designing the basketball shoe in America, Nike's design team made sure that it was suitable for an indoor game, since that's what most people in America play. However, when designing a basketball shoe for China, Nike had to change the sole of the shoe to make sure it would work well in outdoor pick-up games, which is what how the majority of people in China play basketball.

When advertising in China, Nike is careful to label its products as being "of China," indicating authenticity and belonging. McDonald's has adopted a similar policy, labeling its products there "of China" because they make burgers tailored to local Chinese tastes. Going an extra step, Nike China selects only celebrities who are considered "of China" to represent their brand—for example, Kobe Bryant, an American basketball star who is considered to be "of China" because he has been in the market for twelve years and is well-liked by the Chinese.

Companies like Nike need to continue developing methods of connecting with their customer segments that the customers themselves feel are authentic and real. For this reason, it is important for western companies to give their international teams the freedom to make their own decisions. By giving them some measure of autonomy and trusting them to make smart decisions based on the preferences of the local market, the top leaders will ensure that their teams feel part of the company's overall journey.

How can Nike and other companies maintain a strong focus on designing for their customers' needs? The most effective tools for this strategy are used in human-centered design thinking (DT)—a system made popular by IDEO, an innovation and design consultancy firm in San Francisco that contributed to the design of Apple's mouse. Many companies are adopting DT methodology to ensure greater focus on their consumers during the design process. PepsiCo's CEO Indra Nooyi, for example, has turned design thinking into a strategy: in 2012 she created PepsiCo's first-ever Chief Design Office and invited Mauro Porcini to lead the Design & Innovation Center in New York[5]. When companies embrace design thinking, it transforms the ways in which they connect with their consumers. And as it drives up shareholder value, more and more companies will adopt its principles. Below is the standard design-thinking framework; more free resources can be found online on the websites of IDEO and the Stanford d.School.

---

5   https://hbr.org/2015/09/how-indra-nooyi-turned-design-thinking-into-strategy.

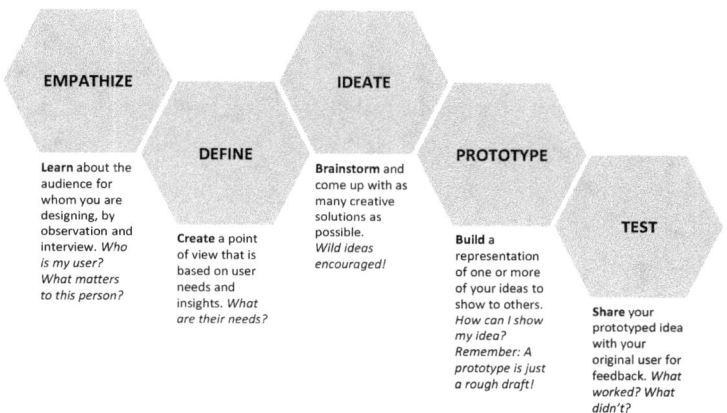

Source: IDEO

Effective design needs constraints, and the following seven pointers help designers as they uncover and analyze customer wants and needs. These overarching guidelines are critical throughout the five-step process of empathizing, defining, ideating, prototyping, and testing[6].

• *Defer judgment.* You never know where a good idea is going to come from. The key is make everyone feel that they can express any idea on their mind and allow others to build on it.

• *Encourage wild ideas.* Wild ideas can often give rise to creative leaps. When coming up with ideas that are wacky or out there, we tend to think about what we really want, without the constraints of technology or materials.

• *Build on the ideas of others.* Being positive and building on the ideas of others takes some skill. In design-thinking conversations,

---

6   www.ideo.org.

we should try to use "and" instead of "but."
- *Stay focused on the topic.* Try to keep the discussion on target; otherwise you can become distracted by going beyond the scope of what you're trying to design for.
- *One conversation at a time.* Your team is far more likely to build on an idea and make a creative leap if everyone is paying full attention to whoever is sharing a new idea.
- *Be visual.* In brainstorming sessions, write down ideas on Post-it notes and then put them up on a wall. Nothing gets an idea across faster than drawing it. It doesn't matter if you're not Rembrandt!
- *Go for quantity.* Aim to create as many new ideas as possible. In a good session, up to 100 ideas are generated in 60 minutes. Crank the ideas out quickly and then select and build on the best ones.

These guidelines not only allow for effective design thinking, they also ensure effective collaboration, a concept at the heart of progress and innovation. Making sure that we pay attention to both our customers' desires and our colleagues' ideas means that everyone is journeying together toward a shared destination—and that means we stand a much better chance of achieving success in the long run.

Case E: Singapore vs. Malaysia

Summary: *Like business leaders, government officials must listen to their country's entire population, not just the majority. Failure to do so is not only unjust but often brings about detrimental economic effects. In recent years, we have seen Singapore listen to the needs of its citizens successfully,* *but Malaysia, in contrast, undergoes difficulties from several disengaged segments of its population, a fragmentation that will hurt the economy in the long term. Whether you are in the private sector or the public sector, a CEO or a Member of Parliament, you must understand the interests and needs of the people you represent. And elected politicians must ensure that everyone they represent feels heard.*

In Singapore, we met with a Member of Parliament and sat in on a weekly "Meet the People Session," where citizens can speak to their representatives and voice their questions, complaints, and worries. I was impressed both by the Member of Parliament, who took time out of his day to listen to his people, and by the engaged young people helping to run the sessions. This group of teens and young adults is more likely to feel part of the community, and by extensive they are more likely to continue throughout their lives as engaged citizens, positively contributing to Singapore as they grow up. Crucially, they are also more likely to want to participate in the government themselves.

The ruling party in Singapore, the People's Action Party (PAP), takes their obligations to the population—all the population—very seriously. They are so concerned about doing what is right by their citizens that they have committed to funding repairs in the housing estates not only for the next few years, until the next election, but for a fixed five-year period, should a different party win and oust the PAP from power.

Many other governments suffer from short-term-ism, in which politicians do what is best for themselves, in their current term, rather than what is best for the people even if it hurts the politicians' own chances of re-election. These officials view being in power as an opportunity to spend the entire budget, so that when they leave their successors won't have adequate funds and will fail to serve the people successfully. The PAP, in a dramatic contrast, have taken the high road and made sure that there will be enough money to serve the people's needs, even if they aren't in power. They have embraced collaboration and inclusion over self-interest, and in doing so they have built a powerful engine of success.

The differences between Singapore and Malaysia were fascinating to witness firsthand. Malaysia is a country with immense potential. Malaysia seemed most developed among the ASEAN countries, Singapore aside, with a stable and extensive infrastructure, highly endowed natural resources, a rich British heritage, an educated population, and a strong Asian base of Fortune 500 global companies. It also has a racially diverse population, which includes a majority of ethnic Malays (53%) and a minority of ethnic Chinese (23%) and ethnic Indians (7%). There are signs, however, that these percentages are changing. A local think tank, the Asian Strategy and Leadership Institute reported that the proportion of Chinese Malaysian in the population would drop to 19.6% by 2030, a drop from 37.2% in 1957, when the country achieved independence.

What is driving this decrease? Simply put, the minority group in the country do not feel heard or seen by the country's government. One major element in their sense of isolation and their decrease in numbers within the larger Malaysian population is the so-called brain drain: many of the minorities, especially the Chinese, are leaving Malaysia and getting jobs overseas, or else remaining in countries where they have gone to do their tertiary education. For example, Australia hosts about 250,000 Malaysian students. Many also leave for the UK and Canada. In all of these cases, the members of the Malaysian minorities feel that they can achieve greater success and find greater equality under other governments.

In few of my discussions with people I have met on the streets, I covered three very sensitive topics: state-led affirmative action, divisive racial comments, and institutionalized discrimination. It was quite surprising and frankly alarming to learn that Malaysia was the only country on the planet to practice a policy of affirmative action for the majority population, as affirmative action is generally meant to support minority populations. I learned that there was a wide range of state-sponsored benefits that the majority Malays were entitled to while the same were not given to the two other minority groups. The second was the frequency of racial comments from Malaysian politicians to garner support from the Malays. From my close observation and interaction with the Malaysians, I could see that most of them, regardless of the race, were very respectful, if not too cautious, to one another. They wanted to carry themselves well, perhaps as a way to not offend others, but to live in peace and harmony with everyone. However, comments that stirred and orchestrated negative racial dynamics, I could see, were generating fear about letting down of the long great legacy they have built together all these while, and doubt about the future they were to work to build together. The last topic was institutionalized discrimination in which positions in the government or government-linked entities were taken up not by the measures of meritocracy, but by quota systems.

The overall theme of our discussion was that the minorities in the country are not treated as equal citizens. In addition to the problematic systems mentioned above, they also have to pay higher taxes and suffer higher interest rates for mortgages. Though *The Straits Times* has declared, "Muslims need to realize that non-Muslims are their fellow countrymen with whom they have a shared stake in the country's continued peace and prosperity[7]," this is far from being a universal mindset, and its lack is particularly evident within the Malaysian governing system. The government has not been so successful to embrace collaboration, thus leaving behind the minorities on its journey toward success, and as a result both sides are suffering.

Malaysia needs to recognize that the minority community has been and will continue to be critical to the nation's development: they are an extremely entrepreneurial constituency that has contributed substantially to the Malaysian economy. The Malaysian government needs to use design thinking both to communicate with all of its constituents, including the minorities, and to formulate methods of devising more inclusive policies for its entire population. It should look to Singapore for an example of putting the population's needs first, rather than benefiting one particular sector. Only in that way will it ensure long-term prosperity for the country as a whole.

Conclusion

The next generation of leaders in the business, governmental, and nonprofit arenas will need to find new ways to solve the challenges facing their businesses and communities. Many of the problem-solving tools of yesterday haven't worked. The leaders of today and

---

[7] http://www.straitstimes.com/asia/se-asia/falling-malaysian-chinese-population-worrying-analysts.

tomorrow, therefore, will need to use both self-innovation and collaboration to keep ahead of the game and to ensure that they are both hearing and serving those they represent.

Because so many companies are fighting for the same slice of the pie, an innovative company hoping for long-term success must do something that at first seems counterproductive to success—they must disrupt themselves before they get disrupted. They also need to take all of their people with them on their journey, so that every player involved shares the same vision, and so that, when as a group they reach their destination, everyone is satisfied.

The concepts of disruptive self-innovation, design thinking, and inclusive collaboration are all crucial in adapting to change and forming strategies for the future, whether you are a leader in a company, a non-profit organization, or a governmental body. We all have many customers, in our home market or halfway across the globe, who merit more of our attention and respect; and we all have competitors who are looking to outpace us and disrupt our strategies. To succeed, we must listen to our consumers' desires and ideas and be willing to reimagine ourselves every day, so that we can stay relevant as we progress. If we can do both of these things, we will ensure a successful and fulfilling career not only for ourselves but for everyone who relies on us as leaders of the future.

| Chapter 6 |
A Comparison:
Policies, Society, and Culture in Asia and Peru

Giacomo Declercq

MIB, Fletcher School of Law and Diplomacy

• • •

It was too early in the morning, and my mind was flooded with a multitude of thoughts as I saw the hands on the clock pointing to 3. Getting up for a glass of water, I realized that sleep was going to elude me that night: later that day, I would be getting on a flight taking me into an unknown future, leaving behind everything that I cherished and was familiar with. Traveling was not new to me, but this would be different. I was going to Boston to begin my Graduate Studies in International Relations at the Fletcher School of Law and Diplomacy. I had always been a fan of adventure, but this adventure involved adapting my way of life and view of the world to a new reality.

My journey's goal was to learn, discover new things, and complement my life in Peru with what I absorbed from each country I visited, city I lived in, or person I met, so that eventually I could translate what I found into some kind of change in my own society. That was my motivation to keep moving and creating experiences to satisfy my wanderlust and yearning for learning.

There are two sides to Peru and two different stories to tell about my birth country. On one side, there is the warmth and innovation of Peruvians, who are a creative people using their imagination and resourcefulness to overcome obstacles. Some of our well-known, unique cuisines, such as the "*anticuchos*" and the "*lomo saltado*," are consequences of the geniality of colonial Peruvians, who improvised with leftovers from their Spanish lords (dishes made of left-over cow parts with rice, potatoes, and other spices). The other side of Peru is the inefficiency in its society, where someone who takes the initiative to do something will ultimately take advantage of others as well. Peru also lacks a solid structure within its governmental institutions, so favors, benefits, and bribes are common. These are the kinds of thing I compare and analyze when I come across other cultures, striving to look at my own country and continent objectively in the comparison. For example, South America is rich in natural resources and people, but the continent is not able to capitalize on growth opportunities, whereas countries such as South Korea and Singapore, though having little natural resources, are able to grow and develop efficiently. This begs the question of why—is it because of the rampant corruption in South American countries, or is it because South American people lack clear national identities with which to develop their nations?

One of the highlights of my time at the Fletcher School of Law and Diplomacy at Tufts was joining the Asia Leadership Trek (ALT), organized by graduates of Harvard University, in which participants of many different disciplines, expertise, and origins are sent to various locations in the Asia to observe the dynamics of growth and development. The ALT program offers first-hand insights through an experiential journey, in which twenty to thirty participants directly investigate political, economic, industrial, and societal issues through engagement with relevant leaders and organizations in the field. The Trek is a prime opportunity for people like me, who come from different continents, to connect with influencers and up-and-coming leaders in the vast and promising region of Asia.

I seized this opportunity without hesitation, as I believed it could offer me a good understanding of what has led some Asian economies to rise while others fail, and also of how these Asian countries compare with South American countries, particularly my homeland, Peru. The destinations—Yangon, Ho Chi Minh City, Hanoi, Jakarta, Kuala Lumpur, Penang, and Seoul—looked intriguing to me, as they showed different levels of development, from the least to the most advanced. Of them, I was especially looking forward to visiting Vietnam, Indonesia, and South Korea. I was fascinated by South Korea because only three decades ago it was a poverty-stricken country, the good twin of its evil other half. What South Korea has achieved so far is no mean feat. I came across a similar sentiment in South East Asia, where the countries often aspire to be like South Korea or Japan.

Another country that suffered at length from colonialism and a well-known civil war, and that has subsequently done well for itself, is the reunified Vietnam. Transitioning from a socialistic government to a more capitalistic economy, it has become one of the most successful countries in Asia. This contrasts deeply with the path taken by South American countries such as Peru, which, between 1968 and 1975, under a socialist government led by General Juan Velasco Alvarado, failed to attain any of the economic growth needed for the nation's progress. Instead it adopted an "agrarian reform," which negatively affected all the agrarian production, resulting in a severe loss in crops and productivity and making almost 70% of the land economically useless. The government decided to distribute the agricultural lands to farmers, giving each of them an equal share of land, but what ensued was national chaos: the farmers were not equipped with land-management skills, and production rates fell, impacting markets for both domestic consumption and export. There was a huge regression in the Peruvian economy, something that resonated deeply with me as I looked at the remarkable progress of Vietnam.

Meanwhile, Indonesia, the fourth most populous nation in the world, with the largest Muslim population, seemed to have something in common with Peru. There was a similarly huge disparity in income and economic centralization in urban areas. Just as all major economic activities in Peru are conducted in its capital, Lima, Jakarta is the economic center of Indonesia. I realized that in both countries there is a stark difference between the capital and the provincial regions. Economic activities and opportunities are highly restricted in the non-capital areas, incentivizing people to swarm into the city. In Peru, this has led to a third of the Peruvian population residing in the capital, causing overpopulation, increased crime, and income inequality. Given that both countries have reached a similar level of socioeconomic development, this was an interesting observation to make.

Visiting the most prosperous country on the list, South Korea, made me think about how it was able to reconstruct itself after being colonized by Japan for more than three decades and enduring a devastating war. Now it has become one of the most important economic powerhouses in Asia. Until the early 1980s, Peru had a higher level of gross domestic product (GDP) per capita than South Korea.

Now, thirty-five years later, South Korea is the twelfth largest economy in the world, home to innovative corporations such as Samsung and Hyundai. On the Trek I learned that quality in education and a strong national mentality have played a major role behind these successes. Peru, by contrast, still lacks the focus and planning needed for developing new industries; it still prioritizes commodities and lacks strong policies when it comes to industrial development.

Vietnam

We landed at Ho Chi Minh City on December 31, 2016, and it was exciting for me to compare the Vietnamese traditions of celebrating their new year with the traditions of Peru, where the celebrations reflect what is coming in the new year. Immersing myself in Vietnam's intricate history seemed to be the right thing to do at the start of our journey. Our first activity was to visit the unnerving Cu Chi Tunnels, a labyrinth of underground tunnels used by Viet Cong guerrillas as living quarters and hideouts from their enemies. Impressive and unbelievable, the tunnels show the Viet Cong's commitment and audacity during the war. I contemplated how history was made here and how the identity of being Vietnamese was forged; eventually, the country emerged as a unified nation from the long period of turmoil. I believe that it was not a particular ideology that led them to survive a thousand years of occupation under China, Japan, France, and the United States but rather the sheer will to save their unique Vietnamese identity.

I was growing increasingly curious about how their aim of creating a socialist state led them to where they are today and how they have achieved the fair distribution of wealth and opportunity for all citizens. Peru's experimentation with socialism and, to a certain extent, communism failed completely due to radical policies and no clear political agenda. Communism today stands as a synonym for terrorism. Perhaps possessing a strong national identity, determination, and a clear agenda for how its state should develop allowed Vietnam to chart a different course from Peru. One difficulty that South American countries have is that they were built by immigrants from Europe together with the indigenous peoples. It could be that national identity and a sense of affiliation and loyalty are weaker in South America as a result, making it harder for these nations to progress with a deep sense of commitment. Our guide informed us that the Vietnamese fought to their deaths, unitedly facing a common foreign enemy, the U.S. In South America, the nearest equivalent would be fighting our own neighbors.

So why does Peru lack a proper national identity with which to propel development? Is it because it lacks a common agenda that can unite its people, or is it because its politicians are busy dividing people and causing resentment against one another, which has led to their embracing populism as a means of staying in power? One thing is for sure, in any country: the right infrastructure must be put in place for anything to happen at all. In both Hanoi and Lima, I witnessed highly congested roads brimming with people in cars and on mopeds. People were stuck in traffic, wasting valuable time that they could have used to do something productive. If leadership in these two places worked to implement effective means of transport, there would be more opportunities for the nations to grow and prosper.

In Hanoi, we had the honor of speaking with several senior members of the Executive Central Committee of the Communist Party. They explained to us how their government is organized and the Vietnamese way of running things. The decisions are dictated by the people at the top, like themselves, working from national and regional agendas. Once decisions are made, they are carried out rapidly, in a *blitzkrieg* manner. Of course there are downsides to this method, but it was interesting to see how committed they were to getting things started and completed. Otherwise, it would be difficult to get things done in a large, government-oriented ecosystem such as the Socialist Republic of Vietnam, where bureaucracy is prominent.

By contrast, "getting work done" isn't what you encounter in Peru. Decision-making lies solely in the hands of the regional governments, where—though it might seem like a good idea for leaders to work within their own communities—populism has reared its ugly head as a means of holding onto power, and important work is often overlooked. Peru is blessedly endowed with a great volume of natural resources, including copper, gold, wood, agricultural products, and fish, among many others. However, ineffective use of these resources has led to Peru losing many golden opportunities to strengthen its economy. Still, there are signs that good things are moving ahead of us. Boasting one of the highest growths in the region, Peru is seeing a rapid increase in tourism and the agricultural industry, as well as in mega-scale copper and gold mining. The revenue and profit generated from these have been quickly moved into housing development and public infrastructure. Nevertheless, these mid- to long-term projects will bear the right fruit only if we manage our resources well. The situation reminds me of the period from 1840 to 1870, when Peru's main export was guano, used as a fertilizer throughout the world. The demand was high, but due to ineffective management and corruption, the profits garnered had only a minor, trickle-down effect on elevating the people's quality of life.

My hope for both Vietnam and modern-day Peru is that these mistakes won't be repeated.

Indonesia

A country comprising 17,000 islands with 255 million people, Indonesia is truly a fascinating country. Nature and modern development were the two things I wanted to explore there. After landing in Jakarta, I soon realized that moving around required some patience, as the traffic was horrendous. At the same time, Jakarta is a bustling business hub, where energy and optimism are at an all-time high. I sensed that people were getting their acts together to help rebrand Indonesia to the world, and the horde of new buildings being constructed was an illustration of this determination.

One experience that gave me fodder to mull about was a day excursion that we made to Pari Island. Its beauty is comparable to the Caribbean islands I have visited, and I concluded that one of Indonesia's key strengths is its abundance of natural scenery. There is a tremendous potential for the tourism industry to grow here. If a successful model, aligned with the United Nation's Sustainable Development Goals, is adopted to tap into the benefits of such natural resources, Indonesia will be able to offer fantastic experiences in nature and hospitality. This will create more jobs and opportunities for the Indonesians, leading to higher incomes and better living styles, a better education system, and a reduction in the number of people overcome by poverty. I thought of this as I observed the huge and very evident income disparity in the country. It was encouraging to see the residents of Pari Island looking happy. They were extremely hospitable and made us feel at home. As an economist, I found that this short excursion and exposure offered a steep learning curve.

Later in the trip, we had two encounters with Indonesians that were especially significant to me. One was with Ms. Desi Anwar, Senior Anchor and Director at CNN Indonesia, and the other was at a forum with Mr. Diaz Hendroprivono, Special Staff to the Indonesia President. Ms. Desi showed more optimism than pessimism about where the country is headed; she was confident that it would become the world's fourth largest economy in the next two decades. Mr. Diaz, on the other hand, stressed the importance of Indonesia's younger generation's involvement in shaping the future as well as in grounding democracy as a means of governance. These changes, however, will take time to show results, and another meeting we had, with the law firm Allen & Overy, made me realize that there is a dire need for the Indonesian government to rebrand itself and to create a cohesive mechanism linking the government and the private sector, in order to provide effective and trustworthy governance. To promote foreign investment in Indonesia a great pool of talent in both the public and private sectors is needed, as well as the upkeep of good business practices. Having the right people driving the right things is crucial. This sentiment arose in Mr. Diaz's discussion of the importance of support and creativity from Indonesia's youth and their contributions to politics. In these technology-fueled times, I believe that the future generation is responsible for voicing their opinions and fully utilizing new technologies in order to get their messages across. Given the "population bonus" that this country has, its future looks highly promising.

In contrast, Peru's youth have historically been detached from the country's politics, a consequence of the corruption and inefficiency of our public officials, who are re-elected repeatedly. Fortunately, since 2012 Peruvian youth have developed a more active attitude toward politics, denoting a clear change. This change was inspired by the need to find better governors and to fight corruption. Given this situation in my country, Mr. Diaz's forum was an illuminating discussion for me, especially since I am part of that generation who does not believe in politics but wants to make change in other ways. The main difference between the two countries is that Indonesia already has strong youth participation; its young people have a clear method of expressing their viewpoints in the media and digital spheres. Peru has only just realized the importance of its youth, following the results of the last elections, in which they rose in response to the potential threat of nationalism and the resentment that some people in the provinces were showing toward the government. Now Peru's youth are more conscious of their role and their ability to contribute to their country's growth. Time will tell how their participation will affect the country's future.

Of the countries we visited in Asia on the Trek, Indonesia was the closest to Peru in terms of its socioeconomic development, and visiting it was an eye-opening and enriching experience for me.

South Korea

Even in Seoul's Incheon Airport, I felt a vibe that I had not experienced in any of the other five countries we visited. Things were more organized, starting at the immigration entry point, and when exploring the city later I discovered how orderly everything was, in well-maintained surroundings. The people I encountered were extremely polite and hospitable; though unable to speak English, they would eagerly draw maps for me when I got lost. Seoul's subway system is one of the best and most advanced metro systems I have seen, and it seemed very convenient for everyone to use. One interesting thing that caught my attention was the special survival kits placed in every station in case war breaks out in the Korean peninsula.

The excellent Korean subway system reminded me of a subway project carried out by the Peruvian government. In the 1980s, the government started developing the first metro line in Lima, supposedly a landmark event, to improve connectivity in my country. However, due to bureaucratic inefficiency, the project spiraled into a stalemate and was abandoned. Today the project is still incomplete—a perfect example of the stark contrast between Lima and Seoul and a demonstration of what efficient and committed leaders can do, as opposed to a dysfunctional government. The experience of Seoul's public transportation made me understand the role of effective leadership in providing infrastructure and, most importantly, supporting all of a nation's institutions in order to progress toward a common goal. It was clear that all the infrastructure in Seoul had been planned as one large framework. The government clearly acknowledged the importance of public transportation, and the people supported its initiatives.

Our second day in Seoul began with a meeting with the Honorable Speaker of Korea's National Assembly, Rep. Shim Jae-chul, who shared his perspectives on Korea's role in global politics and the world marketplace, and on the nation's path in moving forward. The difference in public administration between South Korea and Peru was evident. In Korea, public officials are capable people committed to serving the public regardless of their personal beliefs or political parties. In Peru, the opposite is true. Politicians use populism as a tool and allow their political preferences to define their positions, even if it means slowing down the process of management. Political officials prefer to maintain their influence instead of generating long-term plans that will benefit the people. The contrast supported my idea of the importance of effective administration in contributing to a nation's development. Yet in Peru politicians spend all their time hosting events, throwing parties, or giving out free gifts in order to obtain more votes. That is the form of populism that exists in Peru.

Korea suffered a war in the 1950s that led to the country splitting into North and South Korea. There were almost three million casualties, and most of the country's infrastructure was severely damaged. The Koreans had no choice but to start from zero and reconstruct their entire nation in as short a time as possible. Now, South Korea is one of the major economic powers in the world. This did not happen by chance; it involved the development of a clear national plan by its government and its people. The public understood what was needed to prosper and played a role in contributing to the nation's progress. The achievement is especially impressive considering that the country is not rich in natural resources. The South Koreans took advantage of what they had and exploited it to their benefit, which is how companies such as Samsung and Hyundai came about.

I recently found something that the former Prime Minister of Korea, the Honorable Hwang Kyo-anh, shared on his Facebook page:

South Korea is the eleventh largest economy in the world, the eighth in terms of exports, the only colonized nation to become an OECD member, the second in LCD production, the first in semiconductors, the only country to achieve both industrialization and democracy as an emerging state after WWII, one of the few countries to have a Ministry of Gender Equality and Family, second to none in terms of security and safety, with an average national IQ of 105, the only country to have an illiteracy rate of less than 1%, and the country with the best IT-based education system, among other things. It is an impressive country, undoubtedly—yet I also sensed that some groups of people in Korea didn't share these patriotic sentiments. Perhaps this is a result of a society moving too fast, making it difficult for some people to cope and find a place for themselves in it.

Not surprisingly, I found many things that the Peruvian society lacks in contrast to South Korea, including a sense of purpose and a collaborative mindset for developing the nation; in Peru, no one has taken ownership of the need to lead and promote change that is appropriate for our society. Nevertheless, some efforts are now being made to generate that sense of unity, beginning with something as simple and unexpected as food. Peruvian cuisine has become a beacon of hope, uniting people and building a sense of community and common purpose. Since the 2000s, an annual culinary fair called "Mistura" has taken place, becoming a national symbol for Peruvians as it helps to bring people together and promote our local culture to the rest of the world. The fair's founding marked the beginning of a national identity that is generating a sense of belonging in our country and engaging every Peruvian in our national development.

In Korea, we also visited the Demilitarized Zone (DMZ), a border that separates the South from the North. I vividly remember the grim and serious soldiers facing each other on either side of the zone. I could feel the tension and see the high level of security, with troops stationed along each side in case the other decided to attack. We learned that the highways connecting major cities like Seoul to the DMZ have concrete pillars embedded in them with explosives that will be detonated if war breaks out, so that the destroyed roads can serve as barricades and hurdles. The entire country has a clear plan of what to do in case of an attack. To me, a foreigner coming from a faraway land, it seemed that the Koreans were always on their toes, vigilant and ready to take action against potential threats and disasters. This vigilance demonstrates how crucial the country's military training has been in instilling discipline in its society. Their alert mindset, together with a strong team spirit, has united all Koreans and encouraged them to do whatever is needed to build a greater future for the country and its people.

Conclusion

The ALT was an unforgettable experience that fed my insatiable appetite for knowledge. It gave me a chance to experience many places and to take from each of them a part of what I saw, making me realize more clearly than ever that there is much to do in South America. The Trek also taught me not to observe only the superficial aspects of a place but to compare and understand the consequences of different governance styles.

The ALT made me realize that Peru must foster a sense of unity as a nation, in order to gain the support of private and public institutions and to develop a national plan. With a collective mindset, I believe that the Peruvian society can work together to become better and more effective. Previously I had wondered what we were missing, considering that we have so many resources. Now I believe that what we lack is this sense of unity and collectiveness. Peruvians have learned to take care only of themselves as individuals, forgetting that a society must be built upon community support and a collective plan. Many of our public officials are ineffective, and there is no clear plan for their institutions. The citizens also do not try hard enough to be active citizens, as there is no collective mindset.

Nevertheless, I know that things are changing. It has been a long journey, but our efforts are beginning to bear fruit, and I believe that we can achieve great things if we apply what I learned throughout the trip. It is refreshing to discover that the younger generation is getting more involved in decision-making; people are working toward a common goal; and public officers are collaborating more effectively with private institutions. I know that it will be a long process and that change is not easy. But maybe, if we could see our situation through the eyes of a tourist, we could use what we learn in other places and adapt them to our circumstances.

The whole experience of the ALT was life-changing, and I was excited to get back and share what I had learned. Once back in Boston, I felt a sense of sadness as I returned to reality. The memories of my Trek experiences made me remember my own country and all its beauty. The Trek had taught me how to enjoy the soul of each city in our journey, and I wanted to experience the same feeling in Lima. There are two sides to every coin. We need to have an open mind to understand every situation. I am now more committed than ever to initiating change in my society. My journey is not over yet, as I have a lot more to learn, but I look forward to embarking on my future adventures with a new sense of purpose.

| Chapter 7 |

Does the Global News Media Get Asia Right?

Raza Ahmad

MA, Fletcher School of Law and Diplomacy

● ● ●

I had always been fascinated by personal communication. Growing up, I was very shy when talking to peers. When I signed up for speech and debate in high school, little did I know that I was embarking on a journey that would not only develop my public-speaking skills but also give me insight into international communication among different cultures, religions, and nations.

As a graduate student at the Fletcher School of Law and Diplomacy, one of my concentrations is in International Communications. This field focuses on how information flows shape the way people speak to each other on an international stage. A useful framework used by communication scholars is called the "Alleyne's model." It describes the nature of global information flow, which is heavily focused on the "Global North" (the developed world) and interacts with news from the Global South (the developing world) only as it pertains to the interests and views of the North.

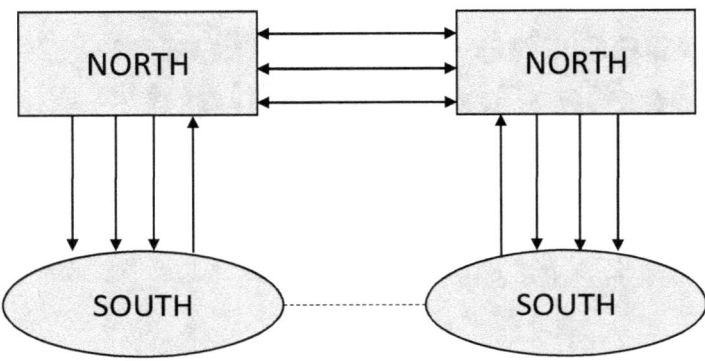

The Structure of Global News Flow

This model in many ways reflects my experience of studying international relations while being located in the Global North. Until I made an effort to learn more about specific countries and cultures from local news sources, the information I received—all from mainstream news—focused on very specific topics and issues, with some insight from a variety of experts. I have actively pushed back against being comfortable with having my view of the world shaped by these information flows.

I have sought to do this through exchange programs, living abroad, reading books and news sources from other countries (in other languages, if possible), and by listening to what my peers had to say. I also wanted to avoid falling into the trap of seeing the great diversity of this planet reduced to abstract terms and entities. When I heard about the Asia Leadership Trek (ALT), I knew it was something that I needed to do in order to further my understanding of the Asian region.

Prior to the trip, I had never been to any of the locations on our itinerary (Manila, Hong Kong, Shanghai, Hangzhou, Kuala Lumpur, Singapore, and Dhaka). Most of my knowledge of these countries had actually been shaped by the international media's coverage of select issues relevant to global news flows. Following Alleyne's model, my knowledge was limited to a select group of "hot" issues: the South China Sea, security, labor abuse, and economic growth in these countries.

In fact, the limited coverage on these countries can be seen in the location of the news bureaus of two major global-media entities—CNN and the BBC. Of the countries we visited, CNN had bureaus only in China (both on the mainland and in Hong Kong)[1], while the BBC had bureaus in Hong Kong, mainland China, and Singapore[2]. This limited focus resulted in a scattered network of news-gathering operations, making it difficult for extensive coverage on the diverse dynamics of these countries to be accessible to an international audience.

With global information flows in mind, I set out to see how the different people we met would present their respective countries' issues and outlooks, while having to deal with the pre-existing notions or images of their countries promoted by the forces of global media.

Manila, the Philippines

The first leg of our tour was to Manila, capital of the Philippines, a

---

1 http://cnnpressroom.blogs.cnn.com/cnn-fact-sheet/.
2 https://www.bbcworldwide.com/how-we-operate/global-offices/.

country that I knew very little about. The news about it in the international media almost exclusively focused on controversial statements made by President Rodrigo Duterte. Our first stop in Metro Manila was the Lopez Museum. What struck me most there was the degree to which Filipino art takes Western art as a point of reference. As the docent explained to us, Filipino art has constantly made reference to ideas and motifs found in Europe or North America, rather than in Asia. One specific piece that I found astounding depicted Spain as a "guiding force" for the Philippines. I couldn't help but feel that the messages presented in the museum were disconnected from the everyday reality of most Filipinos, who presumably do not take such a favorable view of their colonial history.

Another fascinating exchange happened when our delegation met with a group of Filipino Congressmen, including Speaker of the House Pantaleon Alvarez, for a question-and-answer session. Despite the format, it seemed that the Speaker was intent on pivoting to the talking points he had already decided on for addressing an international audience. Perhaps to push back on allegations of human-rights abuses, he argued that the U.S. government's criticism of Duterte's administration stemmed from the U.S. being sympathetic only to the "rights pertaining to criminals and drug dealers." He further argued that the Philippines, as well as South East Asia as a whole, have a "different culture" from the U.S.—one that was continually suppressed by Spanish and American colonialism.

The language of culture and colonialism as a pushback to international criticism of domestic policies is nothing new to me. However, I have encountered it more often in history books dealing with postcolonial nations in the 1950s and '60s. This interaction actually made me wonder if the international media has had a hand in churning out this sort of rhetoric when it takes perspectives from post-colonial nations, or if this was just the approach of a new, populist administration seeking to instill pride among its constituents.

Another stop during our time in Manila was at the Harvard Club of the Philippines. In addition to the participants on the Trek, the guests at the event included Filipino and American alumni of Harvard, as well as four Filipino students who had recently been admitted to Harvard. Over the course of the night, many of the alumni gave short speeches addressing the young students as they were about to embark on their exciting journey. A message that I heard repeatedly throughout the night was that these young students would serve as representatives of the "true" Philippines, and that they would have to challenge the misperceptions presented by the global media.

I can't say I got a full picture of the "true" Philippines from my short time there, but I did feel a sense of irony as we sat in a fancy Filipino restaurant in an upscale business district of Manila, which had been reserved in its entirety by the Harvard Club, and listened to this speech. It seemed to me that this might not be an accurate picture of the "true" Philippines. Hearing from the man at the shoe-shine stand at the Manila airport talk about his dream of becoming a mechanical engineer, having moved from a village in the north to Manila to help his family, yet struggling to go to college due to what he termed a "rigged system" at the top, reinforced my idea that societies cannot have one "true" picture or story. Ultimately, I came to the conclusion that the narrative presented about the Philippines by the global media is indeed very limited in scope, since it fails to show anything close to the complete array of narratives present throughout the country.

Hong Kong, Shanghai, and Hangzhou, China

Our next two destinations were in China: Hong Kong and then Shanghai and Hangzhou. The only knowledge I had of Hong Kong—the Special Administrative Region—was of increasing tensions between local residents and the central Chinese government in Beijing. This had been emphasized mainly through coverage of the "Umbrella Movement," as well as sporadic coverage of tensions between mainland visitors and the more "Westernized" locals[3]. These tensions were often painted as a "clash of cultures", which the global media portrayed as a march toward greater "Westernization" and a mainland government that just didn't "get it." I was eager to find out if this was indeed true or if it was a distorted understanding of a unique context.

One of our meetings in Hong Kong was with the Vice-President for Institutional Advancement at the Hong Kong University of Science and Technology, Dr. Eden Woon. Dr. Woon's own background—he served in the U.S. Air Force, has lived and done business in Shanghai, but currently works in Hong Kong—helped give us a unique perspective into the issues surrounding the relationship between Beijing and Hong Kong (as well as its connection with an American audience). He pointed out that Beijing is particularly sensitive to topics surrounding its sovereignty—a legacy from the colonial era, when Western powers were able to gain highly favorable concessions from China, something still viewed as a national humiliation.

Our meeting with Dr. Woon, as well as subsequent discussions

---

3 http://www.bbc.com/news/world-asia-china-16941652.

with representatives of the Hong Kong Science and Technology Parks Corporation, brought up another important point that I had previously not been aware of: the worries surrounding the economic future of Hong Kong. Hong Kong is known globally for being a financial service hub in Asia. I found out that this view is also ingrained into the local culture; parents actively encourage their children to focus on finance instead of STEM fields, something that came as a total shock to me (among immigrant Pakistanis, we joke that we have only two career options: doctor or engineer). However, while Hong Kong still holds importance in the world of financial services, the rise of mainland China's economy has transformed Shanghai into a new, competing financial service hub. Simultaneously, the rising importance of STEM fields, both in the region and globally, has forced Hong Kong's leadership to broaden its economic focus and begin building a local STEM industry. To this end, the local government has set up the Hong Kong Science and Technology Parks Corporation. The societal focus on financial services has meant a lack of local interest in STEM-related careers, and this in turn has meant an increasing number of students from the mainland filling up STEM-related jobs. It is still early days, but the increasing importance of students and young professionals in a growing sector of the local economy, as well as the potential tensions this could create if wealth or prosperity shifts, is a significant factor in Hong Kong's relations with the mainland that doesn't currently receive a lot of media coverage.

The next leg of our journey took us to Shanghai and Hangzhou, where we focused on China's branding and the growth of the private sector. We had the opportunity to meet with two major Chinese companies seeking to make an impact on the global stage, Huawei and Alibaba. At Huawei, we met with the VP of Global Public Affairs, David Harmon, who had previously worked in the European Commission's cabinet. Throughout our discussion with Mr. Harmon and the presentation we attended, it became clear that Huawei wants to be seen as a private global company, unconnected to the Chinese government. Having grown up in Silicon Valley, where the majority of tech news on Huawei focuses on the suspicion surrounding its wide-area and local-area networks[4], I could see that the goal of the meeting—and one of the key components of Mr. Harmon's work—was to convince customers that Chinese companies like Huawei are trustworthy. The message that the U.S. market is paramount to Huawei was clearly addressed by Mr. Harmon when he spoke about an upcoming engagement with U.S. tech executives. Given the past frustrations that Huawei has encountered in the U.S., particularly in the networking industry, the fact that they are still focused on the U.S. and seeking to change their image in the process was absolutely fascinating.

Our visit to Alibaba had a similar flavor. We were able to speak to some of the participants of their Global Leadership Academy (AGLA), an initiative that seeks to foster "the future international leaders of Alibaba as well as serve as a platform for Alibaba's international business expansion[5]." It was interesting to hear from ex-pats about their experiences of working at Alibaba and living in China. Many of them chose to focus on the language and cultural gaps between their home countries and China.

---

4 https://gizmodo.com/accused-of-spying-huawei-ceo-says-company-is-exiting-1475628703.
5 https://agla.alibaba.com/.

Select Trekkers then ran a variety of workshops for the Alibaba employees. I assisted one of my colleagues, Jennifer Hurford, in a workshop on Design Thinking. One of the tasks we gave to the participants was to choose a problem at Alibaba to address. Some employees suggested the issue of fake or knock-off products being sold on the Alibaba platform, which immediately caused the room to explode in a heated debate. Some employees wanted to discuss the issue of fake products, while others did not want to discuss it in the presence of non-employees. The discussion was carried out in both Mandarin and English, so I couldn't understand all of what was said, but multiple employees commented in English that "it shouldn't matter if we have to save face or not, this is an issue that needs to be discussed."

I was taken aback by the frankness of the discussion, and by how heated the employees became about an issue that I didn't see as too controversial (I haven't bought anything from Alibaba but am well aware of the issues surrounding the authenticity of the products available). While I can't say with certainty whether this incident occurred simply because the employees were reluctant to discuss these issues in front of non-employees, or because we were foreigners who were not supposed to know about these types of issues, I couldn't help but feel that the attitude of wanting to "save face" by not discussing flaws might endanger trust among an international audience.

Another fascinating insight came during our visit to Nike China. Our discussion there turned to the issue of intellectual property (IP) laws in China. There has been a great deal of international coverage surrounding a recent court decision in China regarding Nike's Air Jordan brand and a local Chinese brand called Qiodan (basically "Jordan" written in Chinese characters). Some commentators initially saw the decision as a sign that China was getting serious about protecting IP. However, we learned that there had been a caveat to the ruling—Qiodan could no longer use Jordan's characters in Chinese, but it would still be allowed to sell its products using the transliteration. Consumers who weren't familiar with the actual Jordan brand would still mistakenly buy Qiodan products, harming Nike's sales. I got the impression from our meeting that the Chinese government was cynical in its approach to IP. While laws exist in the book, the sheer size of the Chinese economy means that many foreign companies will seek to enter the market regardless of how committed the government is in protecting IP. This means that under the current set-up, locals are often employed by the knock-off brand factories and Chinese consumers are able to purchase products they perceive as prestigious. Given these positive results, why would the Chinese government go after domestic knock-off brands, especially since they know foreign entities will seek to operate within its borders regardless of its stance? I'm fascinated to see which discourse surrounding China—the lack of IP protection or the large size of the economy—will generate greater interest in the global media.

Kuala Lumpur, Malaysia

As with the previous countries, I had very little knowledge of Malaysia before this trip. In fact, I had even less knowledge about it than the others. It isn't normally in the headlines of major American news channels, nor is it often featured in American movies or TV shows. Neither CNN nor the BBC has any bureaus in the country. I thus went into the country with very few pre-existing notions—outside of its being a Muslim-majority nation.

During our time in Malaysia, we made a fascinating visit to a Chinese-language newspaper, the Sin Chew Media Corporation. Here I learned about the racial and ethnic divisions among the three largest communities in Malaysia (Malay, Chinese, and Indian), which I had previously been unaware of. From what I understood, the core of the conflict derives from the distribution of economic and political power; while the Chinese community has historically been economically powerful in Malaysia, the larger population of Malays, as well as identity politics that pit the ethnic groups against each other, led to the government favoring the Malay population. Unfortunately, due to the limited time I spent there, I didn't learn much about the views and issues surrounding Malaysia's Indian community. Through our interaction with Sin Chew's management, however, I learned about the Chinese community in Malaysia and how they have built different institutions to preserve their values, including schools, media groups, and cultural organizations. Interestingly, despite the aforementioned tensions, there has been an increased interest among non-Chinese Malaysians in attending Mandarin-based schools, partly because of the perception of incompetence in the public school system and of the higher quality of the Chinese system. Another possible reason, which might signal a larger shift in Asia's narrative, is mainland China's rising clout in the region.

We also visited an organization called the Yayasan Chow Kit, which focuses on helping stateless and refugee children in Malaysia. Malaysia's refugee population is quite large, a result of there being a UNHCR office in the country.[6] The refugees come from Myanmar (particularly the Rohingyas), Sri Lanka, Iraq, Afghanistan, and even Palestine. When the global media covers refugees, Malaysia is generally not their main focus. Since there is more media focus on the crisis in the Mediterranean, global audiences tend to associate refugees and migrants almost exclusively with Europe (and, to a lesser extent, the U.S.). It turns out that, unlike many European countries, Malaysia serves only as a transitional point for refugees. This means that refugee families there are largely waiting to be resettled to a third country and lack access to critical resources, such as education or public health services. There are almost 160,000 refugees in Malaysia currently confirmed by UNHCR, with an estimate of more than double that number for those not confirmed.[7] It was heartbreaking to hear about these families' experiences, particularly those of the young children, who in some instances had been orphaned or trafficked by transnational criminal groups into Malaysia. It made me think of the amount of information that isn't coming from the region due to the lack of global media focus on Global South-to-South issues.

The UNHCR is currently worried about the new American administration contemplating cuts to funds and grants that assist NGOs like Yayasan Chow Kit. I could imagine the outrage that would erupt back in the U.S. over cutting assistance to innocent children—if only the American public knew about the issue.

---

6 https://sg.news.yahoo.com/malaysia-unique-refugee-crisis-031023087.html.
7 ibid.

Singapore

Before joining the Asia Leadership Trek, I had some idea of what to expect in Singapore, as I had considered attending graduate school there. I assumed that it would it would be similar to China, with limited democratic engagement permitted by the government. This view was partly shaped by videos and articles I'd consumed that discussed the "economic models of the future" and used China and Singapore as models of managed, authoritarian capitalist systems.

During my time in Singapore on the Trek, I was surprised by the level of civic engagement permitted in the country. We had the opportunity to attend a weekly "Meet the People" session held by Dr. Tan Wu Meng, a local Member of Parliament (MP) for the Jurong Group Constituency, to address complaints and questions regarding government services. The degree of civic engagement and the willingness of the MPs to engage with their constituents, both in a group and one-on-one, was a surprise. While I am not sure if mass rallies or other forms of more organized engagement are permitted in Singapore, it definitely wasn't anything like China in this regard. Government officials were more willing to engage openly with us, answer our questions on the problems and issues surrounding Singapore's governance, and address government policies designed to deal with the diverse ethnic and racial groups in their country. Dr. Tan had previously lived in the United Kingdom, and his familiarity with dealing with foreign audiences and their impressions of Singapore might have also helped him to communicate his government's policies and objectives to us.

The "Meet the People" session was held in an office within an apartment block. Volunteers, mainly young people, helped draft letters for constituents who were having administrative issues (e.g. a passport that hadn't been issued) with government agencies. Dr. Tan was going around the room and speaking to the constituents individually as they received assistance. I noticed that many of them were elderly. Dr. Tan later pointed out that young people who have issues with government agencies tend to submit their questions online, while the "Meet the People" sessions mainly attract elder residents less familiar with technology. The incorporation of feedback from constituents and the youth involvement in the session both impressed me, as did the evident level of pride in civic engagement felt by everyone present.

We then went to the headquarters of Dr. Tan's political party (and Singapore's governing party), the People's Action Party (PAP). There was something uplifting about the PAP headquarters, which was located in a typical residential neighborhood, without much pomp or grandeur. The PAP was founded by Lee Kuan Yew and has governed Singapore since 1959. We had a meeting with the Minister of State, Dr. Janil Puthucheary, who was very open to our delegation's questions regarding policy-making in Singapore. The topics of discussion ranged from the policy of recording each resident's ethnicity (something that would be relatively taboo in the U.S.), as a means of fostering inclusive housing policies and avoiding racial segregation, to Singapore's policy of not allowing dual nationality (to preserve its "unique national character"). As a student of law and diplomacy, I was struck by the two values that Dr. Puthucheary named as defining Singapore's foreign engagement: a rules-based international system and the maintenance of friendly relations with its immediate neighbors.

As fascinating as our interactions with the Singaporean government were, it was difficult to draw conclusions or insights about how its governance model would work in other contexts—developing or developed. Singapore is a very small country, and almost 80% of its population lives in public housing, something unthinkable in the U.S. It is also a very new country, with a new identity; up to now it hasn't had an "aristocratic" class (in contrast with the Philippines, where most politicians came from multigenerational "political families"). This may make it easier for civil servants and new politicians to enact pragmatic policy changes without the degree of resistance that would be present in other countries. Nevertheless, I'm convinced that any policy-maker must study the history and context of Singapore's governance to gain valuable tips on serving the population in a pragmatic manner.

Bangladesh

Of all the countries on our trip, Bangladesh was the only one with which I had a personal relationship, albeit marginally. As the child of immigrants from Pakistan, I have had some experience in traveling to South Asia and experiencing the culture and chaos of the region. Bangladesh fought a war to gain independence from Pakistan a mere forty-six years ago, and the legacy of the war has left lingering tensions. I was actually unaware of how sensitive these matters were until one of my colleagues from Bangladesh told me that it would be best if I didn't emphasize my heritage, as it might bring suspicion upon our group—particularly in our meetings with government officials.

When we landed in Dhaka, many aspects of being in Bangladesh felt oddly familiar to me, thanks to the time I had spent in Pakistan. The crowded cities, the architecture, the intensity of the traffic—these similarities, however superficial, made me feel less out of place.

We were in Dhaka for only two complete days. Despite our short stay, we were still able to attend multiple meetings, in which the issues of information flows and nation branding repeatedly came up. On our first day, we met with the Information and Communication Technology (ICT) ministry, specifically the LICT Department ("Leveraging ICT for Growth, Employment, and Governance"). The officials talked about their goal to increase the ICT sector's importance in the country. While they did describe certain issues pertaining to infrastructure and capital as holding the sector back, they emphasized that one of the biggest impediments for Bangladesh is how foreigners viewed their country. Despite the fact that Dhaka has faced fewer security-related incidents in the recent past than London or Paris, foreign investors and multinational corporations are far more reluctant to do business there, due to the negative perception of its security. The officials emphasized this point, but it was striking that they didn't mention any policies or methods that the government might adopt to change this.

It was also interesting to meet with officials from the Jamuna Group, a large conglomerate with interests in multiple industries, including textiles, chemicals, leathers, and motorcycles, as well as media and advertising. Our meeting was held at Jamuna Future Park, the group's large complex, which includes a theme park, a massive mall, and a TV station. Our hosts were very hospitable, serving us food and drinks (despite the fact that many of them were fasting for the holy month of Ramadan) and insisting that we drink the coffee they had made for us (I don't drink coffee, so when they insisted and wouldn't leave until I was finished, I had to drink the first and possibly last cup of coffee in my life).

During their presentation, I picked up a point that our hosts were keen on making throughout—that their work contributes to the "development" of Bangladesh. They pointed out that their factories create jobs, their malls allow local residents to be part of a consumer experience common in many developed nations, and their theme park offers the kind of entertainment previously only accessible to those who could afford to travel abroad. I had a hard time wrapping my head around how building malls and theme parks could be considered "development." While I can see how the presence of such buildings might serve as a benchmark of a country's income level, the group seemed to be arguing that their projects were the actual development that the country needed.

Two days was definitely not enough time for me to understand the discourse in Bangladesh surrounding development, but I'm inclined to think that the need to project a different image in global news flows was a factor in linking development with a large entertainment complex. Shopping malls, entertainment parks, and nightclubs are all familiar attractions in the Global North, and so they might help to build an image of prosperity in Bangladesh that is both relatable and not currently being consumed in the world's media flows.

Perhaps the most insightful visit during our time in Bangladesh was with Robi Axiata, one of the largest mobile telecommunications operators in the country. We met with their Chief Operations and People Officer, Mr. Matiul IslamNowshad, who talked to us about the various ways in which Robi is attempting to boost productivity and innovation within the company. This includes complete top-to-bottom organizational restructuring, with all positions opened to those motivated and talented enough to apply, as well as the creation of an in-company incubation hub with a year's worth of guaranteed salary for employees who have innovative ideas.

While the company's emphasis on enabling innovation was interesting, my biggest takeaway from the meeting was that our host's focus wasn't entirely on the "branding" of Bangladesh. Robi's dealings take place exclusively within Bangladesh, but by having international investors from Malaysia as part of its ownership group, they imply that the need for "nation branding" is less relevant. Their focus on developing talent within the company, as well as on building strong leadership teams, allows the company to project greater confidence in their own abilities, as well as their hopes for the future of the telecommunications industry in Bangladesh. This is in sharp contrast with the government agencies that are seeking to attract foreign tech companies but are unable to do so due to their struggle to project a positive image of their country. The officials we spoke with seemed sure that this lack of foreign interest was what was holding them back, rather than addressing any internal reforms that could be undertaken to address their failure to achieve their goals.

Conclusion

The Asia Leadership Trek allowed me to challenge my understanding of the countries we visited, while broadening my perspective beyond the news that the international media of the Global North chooses to focus on. While a three-week journey can only begin to scratch the surface of what the region has to offer, it was enough to start breaking down the simplified narratives that I have been presented with throughout my life. I hope to return to these countries and learn more from the people there, and hopefully to help bridge the gaps in our understanding of each other that are created from the one-sided global news flows between the U.S. and Asian countries.

| Chapter 8 |

Vietnam:
Growth of the Lotus Nation

Ralph Poettinger

LL.M., National University of Singapore

• • •

Participants from around the world had gathered for a preparatory workshop in the Taubman Building at Harvard University. I read excitement on all their faces. We were going on a month-long study tour, the eighth iteration of the Asia Leadership Trek. This program is a unique, overseas learning experience devoted to exploring important issues and cutting-edge ideas through engagement with political leaders, entrepreneurs, businesspeople, educational figures, and students. The Trek, run by the Center for Asia Leadership Initiatives, has played an essential role in the Harvard graduate school experience.

Each Trekker was assigned a country that he or she would eventually write an article about. Mine was Vietnam, and the facilitator invited me to contemplate a couple of questions. What interested me most about Vietnam? Why was it important to me, personally and professionally? What was I most ignorant about? Questions that led to more questions…

Vietnam is endowed with one of the world's most varied topographies. After five millennia as a single nation, it was divided into a pro-Western south and a Communist north in 1975. Today it capitalizes on this background as an asset, supporting a strategy by which it sustains an economic boom second to none. The West has started to realize what is happening in China, but the Lotus Nation remains Asia's quiet success story—an example of a country coming together after being divided by two contending systems, a symbol for growth in an era of digital globalization, and a model for following a vision in the 21st century.

I was born in privilege, and my concerns lie in the children I hope to raise one day. To me, Europe's fundamental outlook seems worse, and Asia's better, than that of any other continent. Having traveled from Bhutan to North Korea, and after living in both Singapore and Shanghai, I have begun to wonder if Asia might be the best place for my children to grow up. At the time of the Trek, this question had been lingering in my mind for a while. Keeping it as a background to my thoughts, I wrote down five queries that would form my research agenda for Vietnam:

- How has Vietnam healed into one country in the brief time after its war? (*History*)
- How have its people taken aboard the nation's development strategy? (*Education*)
- Which agricultural instruments has the bureaucracy employed to help this strategy? (*Agriculture*)
- What are the roles of trade and protectionist policies in the strategy? (*Manufacturing*)

- What do Vietnamese people think about their officials? (*Leadership*)

In my analysis in the following five sections, I am applying a framework from my professional background in the private equity industry to Vietnam's national development efforts, with a view to identifying innovative solutions to the challenges that lie ahead for the Vietnamese people.

History

On December 31, 2016, we flew to Ho Chi Minh City from Myanmar. War has been a recurring theme in Vietnam. Streets named after heroes in the country's storied history tell the tale of an enduring exercise in taking on, and fending off, invaders from both East and West. Hai Bai Trung, two sisters, took up arms against their Chinese rulers in 40 AD, and inhabitants of both Ho Chi Minh City and Hanoi remember these warriors when they stroll down avenues named after the sisters. Later, Tran Hunh Dao resisted Kublai Khan's invading Mongol troops; today a boulevard bears his name. Enter Le Loi, a Robin-Hood-like rebel with an ironic French nickname meaning "the law," who defeated the Chinese in 1426 and, centuries later, was memorialized in the name of an artery road. Quang Trung, a merciless military leader in the 18th century, paved the way for many reforms, and Nguyen Thai Hoc triumphed over the French in Yen Bai; both are honored through street names today. Finally, 30 Thang 4 is a thoroughfare commemorating the date on which Communist forces marched into Saigon and ended the war.

I later learned that General Ho Chi Minh thought of the Americans as only one group in a long line of invaders that had come and gone; like all the others, they would ultimately be defeated. Vietnam's history of challenging times has made its people one of the most resilient on earth—a quality they also show in the classroom.

Education

Make A Simple Wish is all about learning. This fascinating organization for high-school students from Ho Chi Minh City, who hosted our stay, brings them out to Vietnam's countryside to meet peers from remote, mountainous, and forested areas. They take with them the most modern technology and the newest learning techniques, as part of a self-developed system called Learn to Learn, which engages students in science, technology, engineering, and mathematics (STEM) in a playful manner. Feeling responsible for their disadvantaged compatriots, these urban adolescents hosted a rural camping trip in Can Gio District to understand the inhabitants' lives there. They collected eggs from crabs and chickens to sell, and they used their profits to bring the students of Binh Thanh Primary School to a 3D cinema featuring educational movies. In Ben Te Province, they used high-tech Legos to transmit lessons in analytical thinking, logical debate, and creative problem-solving, in an effort to guide the students of Le Hoang Chieu Primary School to STEM subjects as a way out of poverty. They also called for donations from their parents, public institutions, and private-sector companies, to offer rainwater tanks to the less fortunate.

Eager to learn from the most renowned academic institutions in the world, members of Make A Simple Wish, aged seven to seventeen, were waiting for us outside the airport when we arrived. Despite our tiring journey, their energy was infectious.

If Myanmar is a country reborn after shedding five decades of dictatorship, Vietnam is a nation transformed by incessant improvements to its standard of living. Food is more plentiful, education more accessible, healthcare more affordable, and disposable incomes higher. Vietnam's people are now well-educated; about 95% of its population is literate[1], and the country's most recent scores on the Programme for International Student Assessment (PISA), which tests reading, mathematics, and science, have surpassed those of Germany, with the gap widening more every year[2]. The nation's egalitarian education system has opened doors for Vietnam's entire population. From 2007 to 2011, more women than men in Vietnam completed tertiary education. Female participation in the labor market has risen to about 74%—among the highest of any nation[3]. And the country's female CEO percentage is the highest in the world.

While Vietnam's prodigious progress is indisputable, the government's towering ambition focuses on even higher objectives[4]: (1) to increase the nation's income per capita to between $8,000 and $9,000 by 2020—more than two and a half times its 2010 level;[5] (2) to transform the structure of the economy, so that 85% of its GDP comes from industry, with high-value-added industries accounting

---

[1] cia.gov/library/publications/the-world-factbook/fields/2103.html
[2] oecd.org/pisa.
[3] data.worldbank.org/indicator/SL.TLF.CACT.FE.ZS?locations=VN.
[4] scribd.com/document/229723594/Vietnam-SEDS-2011-2020.
[5] All figures based on gross domestic product (GDP) in purchasing power parity (PPP) units.

for about 45% of it, and services; and (3) to reduce unemployment to around 3% and build a workforce in which 70% of workers receive postsecondary training, of which about 55% is vocational training.[6] The Socio-Economic Development Strategy for 2011 to 2020 is driving this shift,[7] and the attainment of these aspirations will allow the country to shed its developing-nation status.

Education is key to Vietnam's intention of attaining the status of a middle-income country, as it creates an all-inclusive social fabric that is fundamental to building a higher-value-adding economy. The government spends about 20% of its total annual expenditure on education—more than most OECD countries. Compared to its student body, the country's higher-skilled workforce is still small. Only 6.9% of this workforce have completed tertiary education programs, and only 25.4% have secondary education. These numbers compare poorly to Thailand's 12.6% and 27.8%, or Malaysia's 16.4% and 50.9%.[8] Moreover, because of Vietnam's rapid development, the labor market lacks qualified craftsmen, engineers, professional services workers, and technicians, entailing a skills gap in industries such as electronics manufacturing and information and communications

---

[6] Unlike other places we visited on our Trek, such as South Korea and Japan, Vietnam's population is quite young, which enables the country to go for the long game.

[7] Jackson, D., Beal, D., Malone, C., Tram, N., 2016, Lotus Nation: Sustaining Vietnam's Impressive Gains in Well-Being, The Boston Consulting Group, Inc., bcgperspectives.com/content/articles/public-sector-sustainability-lotus-nation.

[8] Bodewig, C., Badiani-Magnusson, R., McDonald, K., Newhouse, D., Rutkowski, J., 2014, Skilling Up Vietnam. Preparing the Workforce for a Modern Market Economy, The World Bank, worldbank.org/en/country/vietnam/publication/vietnam-development-report2014-skilling-up-vietnam-preparing-the-workforce-for-a-modern-market-economy.

technology (ICT), as well as in the professional services needed to assist the other sectors of the economy.

Two elements account for these workforce issues. First, their ten-year plan from 2011 is the Vietnamese government's most thorough attempt at labor market reform, yet it lacks structured strategies to realize its target of training 1 million workers in ICT and 3 million in finance and banking; nor does it possess an adjustment mechanism for evolving economic circumstances.[9] Second, there is a disconnect between the country's industry—MNCs as well as state-owned and private enterprises—and its education and training systems. Most programs in Vietnam's 460 universities and colleges, for example, don't focus on the practical skills that businesses seek in qualified specialists, instead cultivating more theorists than the labor market can accommodate. The entrepreneurs and captains of industry whom we met on our Trek echoed this finding.[10]

In addressing these difficulties, the country's policy-makers need to focus on education and training, and especially on the STEM skills required by employers. While vocational schools champion learning in these fields, the comments we heard from several members of Make A Simple Wish indicate that many students still look upon vocational training as a last resort.

In the near future, massive open online courses may be able to bridge these skills gaps, especially in rural regions, by digitizing the existing opportunities for vocational training, standardizing qualifications, and distributing them nationwide at low cost. As a mid-term

---

9 scribd.com/document/229723594/Vietnam-SEDS-2011-2020.
10 Bodewig, C. et al. (2014).

measure, existing school infrastructures can be leveraged through face-to-face vocational teaching taking place at the schools on evenings and weekends, which would avoid clashes with regular schooling and also meet the working population's scheduling requirements. In the long term, vocational training could evolve to be part and parcel of the country's schooling system—as in Germany, where two in three youths receive vocational training as part of their school education, both in specialized schools and in companies that take on trainees. These schools and companies teach the students broad-based knowledge as well as trade skills and enable them to qualify for jobs in more than 350 recognized professions.

Agriculture

The Make A Simple Wish group understands that a nation cannot become better with its countryside left behind. The World Bank estimates that a fifth of Vietnam's 93 million inhabitants live in poverty—a number that increases by about 950,000 people (roughly 1%) annually. The median age of this group is 31, and this age is falling further.[11]

After the War, the Vietnamese were on the brink of starvation. Since then, agricultural policies have been fruitful, and the egalitarian land reform enacted under Doi Moi[12] from 1986 onward has made the country into a food-security success story. Steady steps forward in

---

11 data.worldbank.org/country/Vietnam.
12 "Doi Moi" means "renovation" or "to change to something new." It was a policy instituted to move Vietnam from a centrally planned economy to a market-oriented one.

family farming, followed by intensification through mechanization in the 1990s, have enabled Vietnam to pare back poverty, phase out famine, and secure social sustainability, while becoming one of the leading exporters of both rice and coffee.

Joe Studwell in *How Asia Works* argues that Northeast Asian countries like Japan, South Korea, and China have enjoyed greater success in their economic development than Southeast Asian countries such as Indonesia, Thailand, the Philippines, and Malaysia. He argues that the Northeast Asian countries have enacted a set of highly successful policies in land reform, export manufacturing, and financial protectionism. Geographically, Vietnam is part of Southeast Asia, but economically it seems closer to China than to any of its Southeast Asian peers. Thus far, its choices in manufacturing suggest that it is following the Northeast Asian trend, and the implementation of value-enhancement strategies will determine whether it can avoid the Southeast Asian middle-income trap.[13]

Manufacturing

The Korean company Hyundai-Kia is the largest buyer of Vietnamese original equipment parts in the country's automotive sector, which is the second-least developed in ASEAN, coming in just above the Philippines.[14] The free-trade agreement between Vietnam and South Korea implemented in 2015 is likely to strengthen this

---

13 Studwell, Joe. *How Asia Works: Success and Failure in the World's Most Dynamic Region* (Grove Press, 2014).
14 Presentation by The Boston Consulting Group on Jan 4, 2017, in Ho Chi Minh City.

relationship. The year before, the Koreans overtook Japan as the top foreign direct investor in Vietnam, where Samsung alone has pledged to invest more than $12 billion.

I was curious, as we walked into the Saigon Hi-Tech Park for a meeting with the complex's senior leadership, about whether the Koreans thought that Vietnam would win the race to become the global manufacturing and assembly hub in Southeast Asia. I learned that they do, and that their confidence is supported by research from BCG (The Boston Consulting Group). Arguably, however, this success should not be left to foreign companies finding favorable conditions in the country's industry parks. My native Austria is one of the prime places of residence for the automotive industry, confirming my assessment that domestic small-scale operations in this sector can propel technological savviness and widespread prosperity. In this regard, Vietnam should learn from where I come from.

Its uphill battle to gain foreign direct investments (FDI) and to export manufactured goods has been going well, with heightened success since joining the World Trade Organization in 2007. Balanced growth, with a focus on telecommunication devices, computers, and electronic equipment, is its catalyst. Together with textiles, garments, and footwear, these groups account for about half of the country's exports. Roughly two thirds of all Vietnamese exports were aided by FDI manufacturing.[15] Exports have risen each year at an average of

---

[15] Total exports of about $150 billion in 2014, thereof $94 billion. Malone, C., Heng, S.L., Vu, T., Kyaw, K.K., 2016, *Vietnam and Myanmar Continue to Advance,* The Boston Consulting Group, Inc. bcgperspectives.com/content/articles/globalization-growth-vietnam-myanmar-continue-advance.

21% for more than a quarter century,[16] with more than half of all FDI inflows representing labor-intensive manufacturing.[17] Recent global economic headwinds have largely bypassed the country's resilient economy, which can also count on robust domestic consumption against the background of a trajectory growing ever steeper.[18]

Yet the country's FDI economy, while booming, may not be a sustainable backbone in the long term, as domestic industries such as cotton, synthetic cloth, dyes, chemicals, plastics, and steel—all outside the FDI sector—have few supplier relations with it and are serving their domestic market. The spillover effects from FDI include increased access to disruptive technologies and innovative managerial practices, as well as demonstration effects and agglomeration benefits. Japan, Korea, and China have demonstrated that labor costs, low for labor-intensive, low-technology exports, rise alongside wages for more technologically intensive products. However, FDI also ensures the import of capital goods such as facilities, machinery, and equipment, as well as materials and intermediate goods. Adding transportation vehicles to Vietnam's national economic portfolio has completed the country's integration into global supply chains as an assembly hub and a go-to place for manufacturing. On a macroeconomic level, Vietnam's export surplus has balanced its trade deficit in the past, sta-

---

16 Its non-oil export value has been growing by an average of 25% over the last decade.

17 The World Bank, 2016, Taking Stock. An Update on Vietnam's Recent Economic Developments. *Special Focus: Transforming Vietnamese Agriculture—Gaining More from Less,* The World Bank, documents.worldbank.org/curated/en/608961480599012554/Taking-stock-an-update-on-Vietnams-recent-economic-developments-Special-focus-transforming-Vietnamese-agriculture-gaining-more-from-less.

18 Ibid.

bilizing the country's macroeconomic balances.[19]

Vietnam's growth model is losing momentum and, as a result, is shifting from a low cost of labor, faced with structural constraints, to comparatively cheap productivity, framed by a favorable political environment. In "an uncertain world," as Alan Greenspan put it, overreliance on capital, cheap labor, and natural resources, paired with stimuli from loose credit policies and extensive government spending, bears certain risks, if total productivity does decline. In Vietnam, labor productivity growth has leveled around 4% annually, while rates of return to capital have been receding. All the while, the country's environmental footprint has been growing, as it is advances into more carbon-intensive manufacturing, with greenhouse gas emissions outgrowing GDP.

Shortly before our Trek, in October 2016, the Communist Party of Vietnam's Central Committee argued that the Lotus Nation must quickly complete its reform agenda, creating a higher-quality growth model based on enhancing labor productivity, output quality, and the international competitiveness of home-grown companies. In November of the same year, its National Assembly enacted a five-year plan to restructure Vietnam's market economy under conditions of macroeconomic stability, social equity, and environmental protection.

Foreign investors in Vietnam can generally profit from tariff-lowering trade deals, and some get lavish tax breaks on top of that. In 2015, the government streamlined its FDI legislation and sped up permit processing. Even before that, companies like Intel, Samsung, and Hon Hai Precision invested billions of U.S. dollars into

---

19 Ibid.

the country, where factory work is steadily increasing in value. High-tech products as a share of Vietnam's total exports grew by an average of four percentage points annually from 2010 to 2015, and nothing indicates that there will be a decrease in this steady rise. Electronics are outgrowing garments and shoes, industries for which Vietnam was once well-known and which are now shifting to lesser-developed Asian economies.

Before Doi Moi started in 1986, Vietnam was one of Earth's poorest places; it is now a lower-middle-income economy. Before Doi Moi, the country was riddled by inflation and paralyzed by energy shortages; it is now undergoing a remarkable recovery. Before Doi Moi, around 6,000 state-owned enterprises dominated a command economy; that economy has now become an internationally integrated marketplace. Agrarian reforms returned wide stretches of collectivized land to family farmers. Increasing output from this arable land enabled the farmers to send their children to school. With its system of egalitarian education, Vietnam could offer foreign investors a lower-cost labor force than in China, with higher literacy rates. "Vietnam has learned a lot from the experiences of other economies: South Korea, China, and Japan," noted Dr. Le Dang Doanh, Senior Economist to the Prime Minister from 1993 to 2006, in his Research Commission.[20]

Doi Moi led to an equitization process that has increased the number of companies in Vietnam about a hundred-fold since 1986.[21]

---

20 theguardian.com/global-development/video/2010/dec/23/vietnam-economic-growth-development.

21 According to Dr. Le Xuan Nghia, in the meeting we had with him in Hanoi on January 3, 2017, there are around 600,000 enterprises in Vietnam, mostly

The rate of registrations has surged six-fold after the Enterprise Law of 2000.[22] Many start-ups have been born in media, entertainment, and online payments. In my own industry, a minimum of three local venture-capital funds hatched in 2016 are helping to move this market past a previous lack of funding.[23] Craft beer is booming. The dependence on imports from China is declining, as they are replaced by local produce. The larger part of BCG's work in Vietnam already involves domestic companies.[24]

Yet, in 2015, the World Bank still reported domestic private business as Vietnam's sore spot.[25] It is important to remember that China's labor costs are rising, and as it pushes deeper into higher-value-added industries, more of its manufacturing business will be up for grabs. However, as automation advances and 3D printing localizes production chains, Vietnam may be confronted with a dwindling opportunity to position itself as a cheap hub for manufacturing and assembly. It cannot depend, therefore, on becoming the new China in Southeast Asia.

---

private companies.

22 The Asia Foundation, *Vietnam's Economic Development. Private Sector Growth, Provincial Competitiveness, and Best Practices in Economic Governance,* asiafoundation.org/resources/pdfs/VNEconomicDev.pdf.

23 I assume it will also help Vietnam dodge a build-up of bad debt, as has been the case in China—especially as credit-granting is presumably fairly lenient in a high-growth, young-population country like Vietnam.

24 The Boston Consulting Group (BCG) received us with a team of five led by Partner and Managing Director Christopher "Chris" Malone. The ensuing presentation and our talk with Chris were very rewarding.

25 worldbank.org/en/country/vietnam/overview.

Leadership

Politics is a subject for debate in any country, and insiders tend to know more about its intricacies than outsiders. What I learned on the Trek is that Vietnam's government authors more plans than China's. Yet in other areas it is still far from matching China's reach and power. Dr. Le Xuan Nghia quoted experts who estimate the shadow economy as being above 40% of the measured GDP. While Dr. Nghia suggested that small structures in rural spaces rather than underground practices were the best explanation for this fact, in general the Vietnamese officials we talked to seemed cautious about cracking down on corruption in the style of their northern neighbor. Nevertheless, and in keeping with the Chinese model, Vietnam's government must create prosperity to legitimate its very pronounced powers.

Hanoi is a captivating capital. I remember a conversation with three fellow Trekkers when we got there; the city reminded us of China. As if a shadow was hanging over the city, we could feel the complexity of its social fabric. The power of politics in this place loomed like the thick billows of smog clouding the starlit night.

Oscar Mussons, an international business advisory associate with the Dezan Shira & Associates consultancy in Ho Chi Minh City, has said that "[i]t took a while figuring out who was going to be ruling the party in power and who were going to be the ones directing the various departments in the government."[26] The result, according to blogger Ralph Jennings, should shift mentalities toward easier eco-

---

26 forbes.com/sites/ralphjennings/2016/08/10/vietnams-fast-economic-growth-is-slipping-but-no-one-notices/#6370f42078d8.

nomic activity.[27] Be that as it may, an atmosphere of departure was palpable when we entered the studios of VTV6, a national television channel led by famous presenter Ta Bich Loan, who had invited us to go on air as guests of honor in her talk show. The audience in the room was young, smart, and hungry—a reflection of the Vietnamese people as a whole. They wanted to know what the future held for them, so when our host gave me the floor, I gave them the essence of what my career as a value-enhancement expert had taught me.

Looking Forward

Vietnam has faced some of its challenges for millennia. The country is heavily investing in human capital, thanks to rapidly changing circumstances that it must respond to quickly. While the rural sector still lags behind, increasing food security and productivity-enhancing policies have been the fuel for Vietnam's recent growth. Manufacturing has established itself as the next step on the ladder of prosperity. The government plays a dual role as both a pusher for innovation by decree and one of society's most conservative agents. Yet Vietnamese consumers demand steadily rising standards of life. Domestic companies are well-positioned to capture this demand in ways that build value within the economy, but Western expatriates remain role models for building these companies.

While not an expatriate myself, the company I work for as a consultant, Alpine Value Management (AVM), has spent two years analyzing the most effective strategies for the creation and enhancement

---

27 Ibid.

of company value. The resulting AVM Model of Company Value highlights the role of Vietnam's private sector in the country's wealth-building efforts. The model offers a blueprint for attracting investment and talent, as well as a framework for attaining and sustaining leadership within the global value chains of the 21st century. An in-depth understanding of how increasing customer value through business development can lead to company value will enable entrepreneurs, investors, consultants, policy-makers, regulators, educators, and students to partake in Vietnam's progress toward wealth.

In the AVM Model of Company Value, six dimensions lead to the creation of company value, and twenty-seven vectors enhance it. This has been illustrated here in the form of a snowflake:

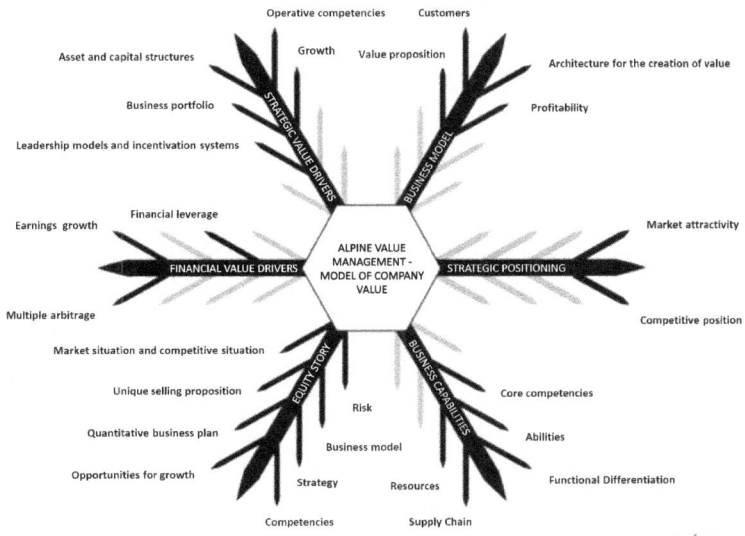

The STRATEGIC POSITIONING of an enterprise is characterized by the attractivity of the markets it serves and its competitive position within these markets. Its BUSINESS CAPABILITIES include its supply chain, resources, abilities, functional differentiation, and core competencies. STRATEGIC VALUE DRIVERS translate operative competencies into lasting value through choices regarding growth, the business portfolio, assets, and capital structures, as well as the leadership models and incentivizing systems that inspire an enterprise. FINANCIAL VALUE DRIVERS enable an enterprise to profit from additional earnings growth, financial leverage, and multiple arbitrage opportunities, in the way that private equity investors strive to do. An enterprise's BUSINESS MODEL connects its customers, value proposition, and architecture for the creation of value and profitability. Finally, these should all merge into one compelling EQUITY STORY that starts with a unique selling proposition, introduces an analysis of the market and competitors, points out opportunities for growth, features a strong business model that unlocks an enterprise's competencies, and balances strategy with risk, resulting in a quantified business plan.

As shown in this model, the creation of company value involves fostering entrepreneurialism and thereby lends itself to learning and training, like any other skill. Vietnamese businesspeople who weave the dimensions and vectors of the AVM Model of Company Value into their thinking can count on leaving behind the command-economy mindset even faster. What's more, domestic first entries into new markets that open up as the country progresses will be able to leapfrog over Vietnam's development efforts, increasing revenues for both Vietnamese companies and their government, as well as strengthening the market positions of home-grown businesses vis-à-vis their foreign competition by becoming national champions in various sectors of the country's economy.

On that basis, Vietnam should identify a portfolio of economic sectors in which it wants to claim a leadership position and then drive the development of domestic enterprises in these sectors. Any such selection should align with the government's focus areas in promoting change. The key questions to keep in mind are how to contribute to development in a given area and which partners would be most effective in making such contributions.

Based on the AVM Model of Company Value, Vietnam should adopt a triadic strategy for building value in its private sector: (1) augmenting the actual, (2) embracing the novel, and (3) initiating innovation. The first can be achieved by pushing established approaches to surmount challenges at an accelerated pace; the second by adopting successful technologies and business models developed in other countries; and the third by originating entirely new solutions to existing problems. For example, in its energy sector, which is afflicted with power outages, Vietnam could develop its distribution networks (augmenting the actual), switch from fossil-fuel-based electricity to nuclear or solar power (embracing the novel), and abandon central energy sources in favor of distributed energy generation (initiating innovation).

Muhammad Yunus, Grameen Bank, and Aravind Eye Care System have all been able to innovate the time-honored business models of their heavily regulated industries, becoming iconic entrepreneurs who have inspired aspiring generations, attracted the attention of the world, and created lasting value for their societies. The BUSINESS MODEL dimension of the AVM Model has dominated much of the recent discourse on competitiveness and value, especially with the internet allowing innovators to recombine the building blocks of business in a wide field of legacy industries. I believe that Vietnam must go for its own 21st-century leap forward—that it must espouse exponential growth by building business models that thrive on technology, thus creating an economy with unrivaled opportunities for the country's entrepreneurs. And I believe that the AVM Model of Company Value delineates the key constituents of this quintessential effort.

In 2016, Vietnam's agricultural sector was devastated by natural disasters such as drought and salinization, which led to an economic slow-down. In contrast, the trade balance swung back from a deficit in 2015 to a surplus in 2016 as manufacturing grew at a double-digit pace,[28] fueled by foreign direct investment but translating into higher household incomes, which underpin private consumption. The fiscal deficit increased in 2016 in line with GDP growth,[29] but the government can draw on privatizations from its pool of state-owned enterprises to balance its budget in the future.[30]

If Donald Trump kills the Trans-Pacific Partnership (TPP), Vietnam can still effectively recreate its effects by entering into the China-led Regional Comprehensive Economic Partnership (RCEP), which includes many of the same members as the TPP but swaps the U.S. for China. While Vietnam's eradication of rural poverty shows no

---

28 Merchandise goods exports rose 30% year over year in December.
29 With an official inflation rate of less than 3%, the government's budget deficit rose from 5% of GDP in 2015 to 6.5% in 2016, according to statistics created by the International Monetary Fund.
30 Focus Economies, 2017, *Vietnam Economic Outlook*, focus-economics.com/countries/vietnam

sign of slowing, it remains attractive for investors, thanks to its low costs, even as export-oriented manufacturing moves up in value through industrial upgrading from garments to consumer electronics. Its population is making more money, and start-ups backed by this new wealth are boosting the private economy. Time will tell whether Vietnam can create significant value from its rising prosperity and reach its goals.[31]

On the last day of our visit to Vietnam, we took in as much of its savory food as we could, lunching like emperors on a peasant's budget. Engaged in friendly banter, we prepared to take off on yet another adventure. Ultimately, I would return to Europe, bringing with me a deep conviction that stagnation is not inevitable. After all, if Vietnam could find a way out of its recent misery, why should the world of my childhood be unable to build on what my parents' generation created after its miserable war? While good fortune is shining on Vietnam, the ravages of time have been eating away at my continent's potential for too long.

When I returned to Europe, it was the coldest time of year. Jack Frost was knocking on every door, sweeping life out of all the alleyways with his frigid breath. Standing on the aircraft's ladder, I remembered soaking up the sun in Vietnam before entering the plane. I could only hope that the change in the weather wasn't symbolic of my homeland's fate.

---

31 forbes.com/sites/ralphjennings/2017/01/05/beer-to-xx-5-reasons-vietnams-economy-will-grow-quickly-this-year/#5f344c222e66.

| Chapter 9 |

What Great Leaders Do Differently, Part 2

Hungsoo S. Kim
MPA, Harvard Kennedy School of Government

● ● ●

As a sequel to my chapter entitled "What Great Leaders I Have Met Do Differently" in the previous volume, Rethinking Asia 3: Social and Political Change, I want to share with readers further elements of leadership, adding new qualities to the list as a result of my meetings with the Asian leaders I met this year. The four additional traits described here are of equal importance to the eleven I laid out in the previous book; they play important roles in the ways that leaders define and exercise their leadership.

12. Character

It was encouraging for me to discover how many accomplished individuals mentioned the word "character" in connection with leadership. Character, as a concept, comprises:

(1) the ability to hold up under adversity,
(2) emotional intelligence, and
(3) spiritual intelligence.

The first trait, holding up under adversity, is the fortitude to withstand difficulties arising from uncertainty, complexities, and failures. Rather than feeling incompetent and defeated, people with character admit their inadequacies and adjust, asking themselves what they can improve to make progress.

The second trait, emotional intelligence, refers to how mature and "people-smart" you are. It means being sensible and attentive to others' needs. Character of this kind allows people to build relationships, understand themselves, and remain aware of others. People with character can manage their own weaknesses, keep disruptive impulses in check, and leverage their positive energy to bring about positive change for others. In two separate meetings with senior leaders from two major global banks, I heard illustrations of the fact that cerebral intelligence is only one indicator of a leader—and perhaps not the most important one; equally critical is the ability to work well with others for a sustained period of time. Mr. Lung Nien Lee, CEO of Citigroup Malaysia, and two gentlemen from DBS Bank—the Group Research Head of Asia Insights and the Head of DBS Strategy and Transformation—all mentioned that their companies were proud homes for capable people who delivered great outcomes, but that the ones who really shone were the ones who embraced a team identity, helping to weather the storms together and producing stellar results in the face of uncertainties and demands. They were the ones who knew how to manage themselves and others by, first, remaining in touch with their own aims and desires and, second, striving to understand and engage those of others.

The third trait, spiritual intelligence, is a form of integrity—a commitment not only to talking the talk but also to walking the talk. The honorable Jae-chul Shim, Deputy Speaker of the National Assembly of South Korea at the time, told us that today's world requires leaders who not only understand what the people need to improve their lives but can also show by example how best to live. This "show me that you live it" code of conduct is necessary in our leaders today.

13. Competency

I wrote about competency in my chapter in the previous volume, but I would like to discuss it again here in order to explain it in a different context. The competency discussed in the previous book involved language proficiency, cultural literacy, and global awareness; this time, I am focusing on it in the light of being work- and people-smart. Mr. Keat Chuan Yeoh, Managing Director of Singapore's Economic Development Board, told us that many leaders today blame external complexities and uncertainties for their own inability to make progress. Real leaders, however, are eager to adopt new perspectives, to initiative new ways to engage people, and to get many things accomplished despite challenges. Mr. Yeoh defined competency as being able to mobilize resources and turn aspirations into reality.

The big question, of course, is how to develop such competency. One of our hosts on the Trek, Mr. Hiroshi Matsumoto—President of Riken, a government agency that promotes the growth of Japanese industry by pursuing breakthroughs in scientific and applied research—told us that it requires preparedness, expertise, and drive. Preparedness to him was a critical element; it requires spending twice as much time charting your new course as it takes to complete the move itself. When preparing, one should ask the following questions: what is required to get the task done? (the capacity); what specific steps need to be taken? (the roadmap); and what will facilitate the process of completing the task? (the resources). Mr. Young Joon Mok, Chairman of the Committee for Social Contribution at Kim & Chang, Korea's renowned law firm, and former Justice of the Constitutional Court of Korea, described this process in another way, calling it the "Have, Do, and Be," or the pre-action stage. A Stanford-educated government official, Mr. Kenji Tateiwa, Manager of Nuclear Power Programs at Tokyo Electric Power Company, whom we met in Tokyo and who played a vital role in reassessing the safety protocols after the Fukushima nuclear tragedy, argued that these preparatory steps were fundamental in establishing whether or not you are fully ready to engage in your task.

Expertise is another important component of competency. I view expertise as a combination of experiences, knowledge, and skills that are necessary when converting plans into action. Together these elements constitute the crucial tools for completing your task. The greater your expertise, the better your performance will be. During the Trek back in the summer of 2015, in a discussion with Professor Kriengsak Chareonwongsak, President of the Institute of Future Studies for Development, a former Member of Thai Parliament, and Advisor to Prime Minister of Thailand, one of our Trekkers asked what competency means in the context of developing countries like Thailand. The Advisor explained that the future of Asia depends on bringing together everyone's experiences, knowledge, and skills, so that we can work together to solve the challenges that Asian communities face. This collectivism is crucial to surmounting overwhelming challenges. In order to succeed, people must own the challenges as if they were the key stakeholders in each issue. When they begin to raise and answer questions about the needs of our communities and our nations, determining what will help and what is harmful, then their positive impact will multiply, and dramatic changes will take place. In this way, the collective expertise of a community can be put to valuable use.

Perspective is another concept that fits well into this context. Professor Se-il Park, a prominent scholar at Seoul National University who also used to work as a Senior Secretary to the President of South Korea, told us that perspective is critically important for leaders, especially those running nations. They need to possess foresight, understanding the main currents of national and global affairs and seeing where their own country's future lies. He argued that a real leader thinks only about making a timely and proper contribution to the nation, using what he or she has been given by the Maker. Without this fundamental understanding of the nature of public service, one cannot run a country well. Professor Park advised us that, if we lack this perspective, it would be better to do something else, rather than pursue a leadership position and risk bringing about negative changes on a broad scale. He also said that, while it is useful to be ambitious, one should never be over- or under-ambitious; otherwise one will fall prey to corruption on the one hand or nonchalance on the other. We must know ourselves, our purpose, and the best ways to improve ourselves at every point in our lifetime. For Professor Park, such awareness forms part of the expertise and perspective that all leaders need.

Dr. Emmanuel Leyco, a professor at the Asia Institute of Management in Manila, defined expertise as "effective communication and reasoning skills," which guide people toward collective progress on solving key challenges, whether they be at the familial, organizational, or national level. By speaking effectively and listening consciously, by discussing hopeful inspiration and by welcoming words of healing, by encouraging others to think about improving our communities and accepting their encouragement in return—all of which require expertise in communication—we can each make our world a better place.

Possessing "drive" means having the energy and passion required to make progress. If preparedness and expertise are the essentials in getting started, drive takes you from one end of your journey to another. Conversations with two prominent Indonesian technocrats opened my eyes to the importance of this trait. One is Ms. Mari Pangestu, former Minister of Tourism and Creative Economy, and the other is a well-known entrepreneur and philanthropist, Mr. John Riady, Executive Director of Lippo Group. Each, on separate occasions, talked about the current challenges and opportunities for their country, as well as lessons from their leadership positions.

Minister Pangestu began our discussion by describing her three handicaps: she is a woman, a member of the Chinese minority, and a non-Muslim. She told us that the key to her success has been her drive, which she has strengthened and exercised throughout her journey. This drive—the yearning to excel, persevere, and deliver—is something anyone can develop. Whoever has a desire can use it not only to their own advantage but to the public's benefit as well. Minister Pangestu's success depended not on her race or her upbringing but on her unremitting pursuit of her goals, with hard work and passion, neither of which money can buy. She credited her drive with enabling her to become the first woman to hold a position in the Indonesian cabinet and eventually to take up two ministerial positions in the government. She gained the people's trust by showing them that she could produce important results in the face of overwhelming demands. Thanks to her self-discipline and perseverance, her ministry and the government as a whole were able to achieve many feats during her time in office.

Mr. Riady, on the other hand, told us that the public will love you as a leader if you embody the ideals you espouse. Many people in positions of authority are good with words but weak in action. But the public is smart, and they want to feel that their lives are getting better; they need to see concrete results. As a result, leaders must implement bold new actions and generate breakthrough outcomes. Needless to say, this isn't an easy task.

I could summarize the key takeaways from these two exchanges using *DRIVE* as an acronym. D stands for "Determination" and serves as the foundation for the four other ideas—for without determination, nothing great can ever be achieved. R stands for the "Right Cause." It is was very important to know what you are working for. Some people end up doing things for the wrong cause and destroying people's lives. We always need to do our research and make sure that our aims are truly worth pursuing. I stands for "Inclusion." As leaders, we must pay attention to people and matters that others would overlook. We will gain greater fruits from our labor if our efforts have a greater scope and include many people in their benefits. V stands for the "Victory Spirit." The people around us should be sources of inspiration for our work; we should help each by offering victory speeches, raising the morale, and keeping the momentum going. Lastly, E stands for "Endurance." Many great ideas never see the light because they are abandoned before they can be enacted. If we see that an innovation will advance the public interest, we need endurance to establish it as a lasting change. Learning to stay in the game is important. People who do so will find great joy in the positive results of their efforts.

14. The Mind and Heart of a Leader

Our world today is in a huge transition. A drastic increase in crimes against humanity, environmental degradation, the emergence of AI, massive migrations, regional insecurity, and widening income gaps are all immense challenges. Everyone today is struggling to meet the obstacles and changes that these problems have posed for us. Dr. Jin Park, a renowned South Korean political scientist, talked with us about the complexities of the struggle to preserve what one values in one's own tradition or culture, while at the same time responding to new circumstances and participating in new relationships. He saw Brexit, the U.S. election, and the new nationalist sentiment sweeping Europe and Northeast Asia as examples of the difficulties of this struggle.

As we spoke with numerous leaders in the region throughout the

Trek this year, I identified a common theme in their words: the importance of developing both the mind and the heart of a leader. To overcome today's challenges, we must possess a strong mind in order to think about the obstacles we face and to devise creative solutions. Having the mind of a leader means being strategic and smart. Having the heart of a leader, on the other hand, means understanding why our thoughts and actions matter to humankind. Many of the people we spoke with on the Treks expressed grave concern about the world's current trajectory. No one could explain exactly where we were going and how our world would look twenty to fifty years from now. In times like this, they said, the mind and the heart are both critically important.

One banker from Hong Kong who spent more than three decades in the industry and whose name he did not want me to quote discussed the 2008 financial crisis. Those who developed and sold the financial derivatives that led to the crash were extremely talented and smart—but they possessed sound minds without sound hearts, and their selfish actions led to the recession. Conversely, with a caring heart but an ineffective mind, a person cannot take meaningful action. For this reason, as the leaders we spoke with told us over and over, both attributes are equally necessary.

Many organizations exemplify this partnership of mind and heart. They nurture their employees and their communities both intellectually and emotionally, and so they thrive. The beauty of this concept is that it can be applied equally well in a personal and in a national context, with families and also with governments. When parents and national leaders speak and act using both mind and heart, their children and constituents see it and respond with equal commitment to creating positive change.

15. Focus & Attention

The last—but not the least—of the four traits discussed in this chapter is the skill of focusing on the well-being of humankind and the improvement of human conditions. At the various startups we visited on the Treks—both for- and not-for-profits, of which two are now unicorns—I could sense the founders' passion and see the fire within their hearts. They shared what had guided them on this journey, the causes they deeply cared about, and the ways in which they were working to advance the public interest through their interventions.

Many of them were most proud of opening doors for people by providing them with employment opportunities. Their work is often deeply influential in their communities, which are struggling to escape the long-standing cycle of poverty: an impoverished generation cannot afford to pay for their children's education, thus ensuring that they too will live a life of poverty. The intervention of the startups has broken this cycle in many cases and helped the locals to find work and gain hope and courage of their own. Dr. Jeffrey Cheah, Founder and Chairman of Sunway Group and the Jeffrey Cheah Foundation, told us that his company is providing employment opportunities, directly and indirectly, for over 25,000 individuals. He stated that young people should be encouraged to find jobs that not only pay well but also address their communities' interests—social-profit businesses that combine economic drive with philanthropic principles. He himself still sees many windows of opportunities for social profit and is already considering a move into a new space, for reasons of the public's interest.

To combine these goals, he said, requires both passion and attention. We need to pay attention to social issues that others dare not consider and then develop a passion to solve them; at the same time, we must stay focused and remain in the game, even if success doesn't come immediately. Without a burning passion to complete one's aims, it can be difficult to reach the end-point. But one encouraging element that we found in all the startups was that, because businesses are almost always digital now and the public has increasingly easy access to the internet, the startups' work is that much easier. They can not only identify areas that might be monetized and work out the financial sustainability of the plan, but also—equally quickly—mobilize the public's interest in the reasons and aims of their work.

For Dr. Cheah, the combination of profit and social activism form the definition of leadership: identifying opportunities that will bring both him and his community lasting benefits. He believes in sharing wealth, hope, and happiness, and I was deeply inspired to see how wholeheartedly he was living his vision.

Concluding Remarks

Throughout the 2017 Treks, I had the joy and privilege of speaking to many successful leaders in Asia. I also took notes on the invaluable lessons they shared with us. They sparked much reflection in me, and now, as I put them into a refined structure for our readers, I am reminded once again of why leadership is so important.

One key point is that everyone can exercise leadership—and it can take any form or shape. The litmus test of whether or not we are exercising it is whether or not we are improving human conditions. When this is done in collectively, both Asia and our entire world will become a more beautiful place. In this chapter, I have shared the elements of leadership that we can find in a person's character, competence, mind and heart, and focus. These were all inspired by the thought-leaders we met along with way in 2017.

A second point is that we can be leaders while still following the guidance of others—you do not have to head a company to be a leader within it. We must understand ourselves first, then pay attention to our surroundings to find out where we can make a timely intervention, and then, finally, invite others to make similar contributions. Together, these three steps form the journey of leadership and bring about meaningful progress. And this manifold form of leadership is what Asia needs. Rather than one person dictating the conditions of our world and our future, we need more dedicated and driven entrepreneurs, government officials, and corporate leaders, equipped with strong hearts and minds. With them at the helm, Asia's people will be able to feel very hopeful for its present and its future.

As you read the following chapters, I hope you will gain a greater understanding of how we can start to exercise leadership by developing a sense of ownership of our future. When we participate in that future and collaborate with others, we can tackle the issues that have captured our attention—or, to put it differently, the issues that make our heart pound and inspire us to take action. On our Treks, I was thrilled to be reminded of how important these efforts are, as we worked to connect Asia with great talents, best practices, and new perspectives from around the world. The ALT, to my mind, is a nearly ideal model for initiating a greater understanding among different people and nations, adopting new perspectives, identifying news ways of working together, implementing bold new actions, and producing outcomes that will bring about positive progress.

Lastly and most importantly, the Treks in 2017 reminded me once again that leadership is something we must continue to nurture. It is not something only a selected few are born with but rather a talent that everyone can develop. The Asia Leadership Trek itself has demonstrated a form of leadership in the development of other important entities, including the Asia Leadership Institute, the Acumen Case Center, and the ACC's publishing house. All of these branches help to cultivate leaders of today and tomorrow for Asia.

Without this work, I would have never had a chance to meet so many remarkable leaders within and beyond Asia in such a short period of time. Every single one has offered me wisdom, insight, and inspiration. I believe that we have more reasons than ever to be hopeful for Asia's people, its nations, and its future as a region, for the simple reason that it holds so many people who are willing to identify problems and create solutions. They possess great optimism for their future, and I feel certain that we can all share their hope.

Editor's Acknowledgments

• • •

I would like to acknowledge the help of all the people involved in the Asia Leadership Trek VIII and Asia Leadership Trek IX, circa 2016-2017, and those who have had a hand in the publication of this book.

Thank you to all the Trekkers, with whom I spent a memorable time traveling and learning in a once-in-a-lifetime journey throughout Asia: Jeff Can Cui, Catherine Yuen, Daiki Tajima, Dang Nguyen, Giacomo G. Canepa, Tan Puay Siang, Jia Wen Hoe, Jasdeep Randhawa, John Lim, Justin Hardley, Chloe Kyunga Jeong, Luis Miguel Cotti, Orianne Montaubin, Phillip Shattan, Rahul Srinivasan, Seokjoon Moon, Ralph Poettinger, Ulrish Kopetzki, Wilson Kyi, Yoshiko Takase, Zhaoying Xu, Raza Ahmad, Benedikt Groever, Catherine Keane, Emily Gannam, Jennifer Hurford, Peter Deutscher, Sheikh Iran Mohammed, Suzuki Soichiro, Takuya Takeda and Yutaro Hokari.

I also would like to thank to each and every one of the authors who contributed their time, effort, and dedication to this book: Umar Shavurov, Philipp Essl, Jennifer Hurford, Helen Van Baal, Tan Puay Siang, Giacomo G. Canepa, Ami Valdemoro, Raza Ahmad and Ralph Poettinger.

My sincere gratitude to the Treks' individual supporters, co-organizers, and partners who were instrumental in helping us to successfully organize our programs in various cities across Asia. The Treks wouldn't have happened without your encouragement and contribution:

Asia Leadership Trek VIII

Yangon: General Thura Tin Oo, Chairman of the National League for Democracy; Ambassador Scot Merciel, at the US Embassy Burma; Ms. Ei Pyho Han; Ms. Andrea Samaniego, AIESEC Myanmar; Mr. Zae Moe, The Assistance Association for Political Prisoners; Mr. U Zaw Min Min, President of the UMFCCI.

Ho Chi Minh City: The student volunteers of the Make a Simple Wish Foundation; Mr. Nam Kahn; Mrs. Huynh Thi Dao Ngi, Chief Operations Officer of TNT Logistics; The staff at Institute for Cultural Exchange France (IDECAF); Mr. Huynh Tri Nhon, Chairman of the Board at Kim Son International Investment; Mr. Tran Van Ly, Chairman and CEO at Saigonlab JSC; Mrs. Nguyen Thi Kim Loan (MD), Head of Hospital HCMC University's Medical Center; Mr. Nguyen Trong Phuoc, Editorial Secretary of Thanh Nien Newspaper;

Hanoi: Madam Dang Thi Ngoc Thinh, Vice President of Socialist Republic Vietnam; Madam Nguyen Thi Doan, Chairlady of the Vietnam Association for Promoting Education; Madam Ta Bich Loan, Editor of Vietnam Television; Dr. Le Xuan Nghia; Mr. Dao Khanh Hip, CEO MAMA Chocolate.

Jakarta: Mr. Dayu Dara Permata, Co-founder of Gojek; Mr. Danny Wiranto, Chief Marketing Officer of GDP Ventures; Mr. Desi

Anwar, Senior Anchor of CNN Indonesia; Mr. Diaz Hendropriyono; Ms. Grace Natalie; Mr. Arya Kuntadi; Mr. Novel Saleh; Mr. Ivanhoe Semen; Ms. Kanti Janis; Mr. Andi Sparringa; Ms. Athika Batangtaris; Mr. Sandiago Uno; Mr. Tom Trikasih Lembong, Chairman of the Indonesian Investment Agency; Ms. Mira Zakaria and Mr. Fajar Triperdana at Polyglot Indonesia.

Penang: Dato' Ar. Ooi Sian Hia, Executive Chairman of Ghee Hiang Biscuits; Mr. Ch'ng Huck Theng, Executive Director of Ghee Hiang Biscuits; Yg. Bhg. Dato' Lee Kah Choon, Director of Penang Development Corporation and Advisor to the Chief Minister of Penang; Yg. Bhg. Dato' Syed Mohamad Syed Murtaza, Executive Chairman of Master-Pack Group Berhad; Yg. Bhg. Professor Dr. P. Ramasamy Palanisamy, Deputy Chief Minister of Penang; Dr. Mary Ann Harris, President of the Penang Centre of Education Tourism; Mr. Ooi Chok Yan, CEO of Penang Global Tourism; Professor. Dato' Dr. Ahmad Shukri Mustapha Kamal, Vice-Chancellor of University Sains Malaysia (USM); Mrs. Ahila Ganesan, General Manager of Sunway Property.

Kuala Lumpur: Professor Leong Choon Heng, Deputy Director of the Jeffrey Sachs Center at the Sunway University; Dr. Elizabeth Lee, Senior Executive Director of Sunway Education Group; Professor Graeme Wilkinson, Vice Chancellor of Sunway University; Mr. Evan Cheah, CEO of Sunway Ventures; Dr. Ramon Navaratnam, Corporate Advisor, Sunway Group; Mr. Tan Kia Loke, Senior Managing Director, Chairman's Office Sunway; Group Ms. Sarena Cheah, Managing Director of Property Development Division for Malaysia and Singapore, Sunway Group; Yg. Bhg. Dato' Sri Mustapa Mohamed, Minister of International Trade and Industry Mr. Wan Khye

Theng, Operations Manager of GrabCar, Mr. Saiful Azhar Shaharun, Senior Assistant Secretary to Prime Minster Dato' Sri Najib Razak; Tan Sri Dato' Azman Mokhtar, CEO of Khazanah Nasional Berhard; Mr. Michael Quinlan, Cultural Affairs Officer, The US Embassy Kuala Lumpur; All Volunteer Teaching Assistants and Interns of Sunway Education Group.

Seoul: Mr. Shim Jae-chul, First Deputy Speaker of Parliament; Mr. Casey Lartigue, Co-founder of Teach North Korean Refugees Organization;

Tokyo: Mr. Kenji Tateiwa, Manager of Nuclear Power Programs at the Tokyo Electric Power Company; Mr. Hiroshi Matsumoto, President of RIKEN Research;

Asia Leadership Trek IX

Manila: Mr. Suchin Teoh, Country Specialist of the Asian Development Bank; Mr. Sung Kim, The US Ambassador to the Philippines; Mr. Pantaleon Alvarez, Speaker of the Philippines Congress; Mr. Anders Baerlund, Partner at McKinsey Philippines, Mr. Tony Abad, Anchor at Bloomberg Philippines, Mr. Victor Manhit, President of Stratbase ADRI; Mr. Albert Del Rosario, Former Foreign Affairs Secretary; Dr. Edgardo Rodriguez, President of Enderun Colleges.

Hong Kong: Mr. Fergus Fung, Executive Director of Lan Kwai Fong Group;; Dr. Eden Woon, Vice President of Hong Kong University of Science and Technology; Mr. Albert Wong, CEO of Hong Kong Science and Technology Park

Shanghai: Mr. Eric Lee, CEO and President of Anomaly Shanghai;

Mr. David Harmon, Vice President of Global Public Affairs of Huawei; Mr. Gavin Lindberg, CFO and Vice President of NIKE Greater China; Mr. James T. Arredy, Journalist from Wall Street Journal; Mr. Benjamin T. Wood, Principal of Shanghai Studios.

Kuala Lumpur: Dr. Elizabeth Lee, Senior Executive Director of Sunway Education Group; Yg. Bhg. Dato' Seri Mohamed Hassan Md. Kamil, CEO of Takaful Malaysia, Dr. Hartini Zainudin, Founder of Yayasan Chow Kit; Tunku Zain Abidin, Trustee of Yayasan Chow Kit; Mr. Kuik Cheng Kang, Executive Editor in Chief of Sin Chew Media; Mr. Lee Lung Nien, CEO of Citibank Malaysia; All Volunteer Teaching Assistants and Interns of Sunway Education Group.

Singapore: Mr. Janil Puthucheary, Minister of State People's Action Party (PAP); Mr. Bilahari Kausikan, Ambassador-at-Large and Policy Advisor at the Ministry of Foreign Affairs.

Dhaka: Mr. Anir Chowdhury, Head of UNDP Access to Information (a2i), Project of the Prime Minister's Office; Mr. Rezaul Karim, Director of LICT Project; Mr. Sami Ahmed, Component Team Leader, Information and Communication Technology, LICT Project; Mr. Tyseer Amin, Senior Facilitator of Standard Chartered Bangladesh Learning Academy; Mr. Rex Moser, Public Affairs Officer at the US Embassy in Bangladesh; Mr. Robi Nowshad, CEO of Axiata Limited; Mr. Nahiyan Naser, Presenter at Radio Next; Dr. Saiful Majid, Director of University of Dhaka Institute of Business Administration; Mr. Rashedul Hossain, Country Manager of MicroEnsure; Mr. Mark Pierce, Country Director of Save the Children; Mr. Sheikh Mohammed Irfan.

I wish to express my sincere appreciation to Ms. Rajeswari Ramanee, Manager of Acumen Case Center & Publishing at CALI Malaysia for overseeing the content and applying editorial best practices in this book.

I am truly overwhelmed by the support of my brilliant team at CALI Boston, Ms. Ursula DeYoung, Advisor of Publication Affairs, and CALI Malaysia: Dr. Gin Chee Tong, Head of Strategy and Management; Ms. Erin Ng, Lead of Creative Design and Social Media; Ms. Selma Bardakci, CALI-Atlas Corps Fellow of International Affairs; Ms. Farzeera Emir, Senior Lead of Planning and Management and Executive Assistant to President; and the Center's interns, Kajendra Govindasamy and Jynice Ong, who worked hard toward the successful publication of this book.

Thank you everyone for your assistance, generosity, and commitment.

| Appendix I |
Trek and Fellowship Itinerary

••

Asia Leadership Fellowship 2017

Date	Events
July 1, 2, 15, 16, 23 and 30	**Asia Leadership Youth Program** Asia Leadership Conference. Developing a Personal Brand Kuala Lumpur, Malaysia
July 10 - 14	**Asia Leadership Youth Program** Asia Leadership Youth Camp. Developing 21st Century Core Competencies Kuala Lumpur, Malaysia
July 17 – 21	**Asia Leadership Executive Program** Executive Leadership School: Harvard's Way of Developing a Talent Kuala Lumpur, Malaysia
July 24 – 28	**Asia Leadership Youth Program** Asia Union Leaders Summit Seoul, Korea
August 1 – 3	**Asia Leadership Executive Program** Adaptive Leadership: Mobilizing Teams for Change Kuala Lumpur, Malaysia
August 11	**Asia Leadership Executive Program** Mobilizing Teams for Change Manila, Philippines

August 14-18	**Asia Leadership Youth Program** Developing a Powerful Personal Brand Beijing, China
September 9-10	**Asia Leadership Executive Program** Adaptive Leadership Workshop Bishkek, Kyrgyzstan
September 29-30	**Asia Leadership Executive Program** Philippine Emerging Leaders Initiative Manila, Philippines
November 7-9	**Asia Leadership Executive Program** Perspective Leadership: Character Courage and Commitment Kuala Lumpur, Malaysia

● ● ●

Asia Leadership Trek 2017

Tuesday, December 27

Arrival in Myanmar from Boston

Wednesday, December 28

8.45am	Meeting at UNESCO Center for Business Development
11.00am	Meeting with General Thura Tin Oo at National League for Democracy
3.00pm	Dialogue with Amb. Scot Marciel at US Embassy
7.00pm	Meeting with Harvard Alumni and Friends Get - Together

Thursday, December 29

2.00pm	Meeting with Assistance Association for Political Prisoner
5.00pm	Dinner at Rangoon Tea House with local social impact leaders

Friday, December 30

8.30am	Opening Remarks by Andrea Samaniego, AIESEC Myanmar
8.40am	Opening Remarks by John Lim, Co – Founder of Center for Asia Leadership
8.50am	"Making the Most of Opportunities to Have and Unconventional but High-Impact Career" by Jasdeep Randhawa
9.05am	Panel Discussion with ALT delegates Wilson Kyi, Catherine Lee, Ralph Poettinger Workshop Breakout Sessions on Mobilizing Teams For Change, Managing Projects Strategically, Negotiations 101, Leading Global Teams Through EQ, Unlocking the Diversity Code, Managing Difficult Conversation
11.25am	Career Mentoring Sessions on International Development and International NGO's, Think Tank and Policy Research, Being a Woman in a Male – dominated Workplace, Networking Essentials, Building a Social Media Brand, Making a Great First Impression, Preparing for Interviews: Communicating your Personal Brand
3.00pm	Meeting at the UMFCCI with the President U Zaw Min Win

Saturday, December 31

	Travel to Ho Chi Minh

Sunday, January 1

9.00am	Guided Tour at Cu Chi Tunnels

Monday, January 2

9.00am	Meeting with Institute Exchange Cultural with the France (IDECAF)
1.30pm	Meeting with at Vietjet Aviation Joing Stock Company
5.00pm	Travel to Hanoi

Appendix I | Trek and Fellowship Itinerary   229

Tuesday, January 3

7.45am	Guided Tour at Ho Chi Minh Mausoleum
8.20am	Meeting at Vietnam Television (VTV)
9.00am	Show Dialogue/Meeting Vietnam Television (VTV)
2.10pm	Meeting with Dr. Le Xuan Nghia
3.15pm	Meeting at MAMA Chocolate with the CEO Mr. Dao Khanh Hiep
6.00pm	Travel to Tan Son Nhat

Wednesday, January 4

9.00am	Meeting at the Boston Consulting Group
11.30am	Tour of Saigon Hi-Tech Park
4.30pm	Travel to Jakarta

Thursday, January 5

9.00am	Meeting at Gojek Indonesia Mr. Danny Wiranto
2.00pm	Meeting with Danny Wirianto, Chief Marketing Officer, GDP Venture
5.00pm	Meeting with Desi Anwar, Senior Anchor, CNN

Friday, January 6

9.30am	Meeting at Allen Overy, Ginting & Reksodiputro
2.00pm	Discussion with young political leaders on democracy (Theme. The vital role of youth in advancing democracy in Indonesia)
5.30pm	Dinner and discussion hosted by Sandiaga Uno, Chairman of the Indonesian Investment Agency

Saturday, January 7

9.00am	Guided Tour at Textile Museum and Jakarta Monuments
2.00pm	Meeting with Polyglot Indonesia Mixer

230   Rethinking Asia

Sunday, January 8

| | Free Time |

Monday, January 9

9.00am	**Professional Development Seminar at the Ministry of Foreign Affairs**
	Project Management, Lou Cotti; Writing with Impact, Wen Hoe Jia; Negotiations 101, Ulrich Kopetzki
3.45pm	Travel to Penang

Tuesday, January 10

9.00am	Dialogue on Heritage, Business and Interracial Marriage with Executive Chairman of Ghee Hiang, Ar Ooi Sian Hia, Soecuak Advisor to the Chief Minister of Penang, Lee Kah Choon and Executive Chairman of Master-Pack Group Syed Mohamad bin Syed Murtaza
11.30am	Courtesy Visit to Penang Deputy Chief Minister II, Y.B. Prof. Dr. P. Ramasamy A/L Palanisamy
2.00pm	Guided Tour at Ghee Hiang and Khoo Kongsi
4.50pm	Dialogue on Tourism, Education & Medical and Art with CEO of Penang Global Tourism Ooi Chok Yan, President of the Penang Center of Education Tourism, Dr Mary Ann Harris and Executive Director of Ghee Hiang, Ch'ng Huck Theng

Wednesday, January 11

9.00am–2.30pm	**Asia Leadership Conference 2017 in Universiti Sains Malaysia**
8.30am	Opening Remarks by Mr Samuel Kim, President, Center for Asia Leadership
	Welcoming Remarks by Professor Dato' Dr Ahmad Shukri Mustapa Kamal, Vice-Chancellor, University Sains Malaysia (USM)
8.40am	TED-style Talk by Ulrich Kopetzki
8.50am	Panel Discussion On Leadership by ALT Trekkers

Appendix I | Trek and Fellowship Itinerary 231

9.45am	Workshops facilitated by ALT Trekkers
11.15am	Professional Development Seminars OR U.S. University Admissions
12.05pm	TED-style Talk- Rahul Srinivasan
12.15pm	Closing Remarks
12.20pm	Lunch + Networking hosted by USM
3.00pm	Meeting with General Manager of Sunway Property, Ahila Ganesan

Thursday, January 12

8.00am	Travel to Kuala Lumpur
12.30pm	Meeting and lunch with Minister of International Trade and Industry, Y.B. Dato' Sri Mustapa Mohamed
3.00pm	Meeting with Operations Manager of GrabCar, Wan Khye Theng
5.00pm	Welcome Tea hosted by Sunway Education Group
7.30pm	Dinner hosted by Senior Assistant Secretary to Prime Minister Najib Razak, Saiful Azhar Shaharun

Friday, January 13

11.00am	Meeting and lunch with Managing Director of Khazanah Nasional Berhad, Tan Sri Dato Azman Mokhtar
2.00pm	Dialogue with US Embassy - Welcome from Cultural Affairs Officer Michael Quinlan
4.30pm	Meeting with Sunway Ventures CEO, Evan Cheah
5.30pm	Meeting and Dinner with Corporate Advisor of Sunway Group, Ramon Navaratnam, Senior Managing Director, Chairman's Office, Tan Kia Loke, Managing Director of Property Development Division for Malaysia and Singapore, Sarena Cheah, and Jeffrey Sachs Center on Sustainable Development Prof. Leong Choon Heng, Deputy Director

Saturday, January 14

	Asia Leadership Conference 2017 in Sunway University
9.00am	Welcoming Remarks by Senior Executive Director, Sunway Education Group and Sunway University, Dr Elizabeth Lee
9.05am	Opening Remarks by President of Asia Leadership Trek, Hungsoo S. Kim
9.10am	Keynote Address by Justin Hartley
9.35am	Acumen Case Center Publishing Book Launch
9.45am	Panel Discussion A. Challenge and Purpose
10.30am	Tea Break & Networking
10.55am	Workshops A
12.15pm	Lunch
1.00pm	TED-style Talk by Rahul Srinivasan
1.10pm	Panel Discussion B. Tackling Challenge and Creating Opportunities
2.05pm	Workshops B
3.35pm	Career Mentoring
4.25pm	Professional Development
5.15pm	Closing Remarks by Vice-Chancellor of Sunway University, Professor Graeme Wilkinson
5.20pm	Networking
5.35pm	End

Sunday, January 15

7.30am	Travel to Seoul

Monday, January 16

10.00am	Meeting with North Defectors & Teach North Korea Refugees Organization with Casey Lartigue
11.00am	Meeting with Deputy Speaker of the National Assembly, Shim Jae - Chul

Appendix I | Trek and Fellowship Itinerary 233

12.00pm	Guided Tour of the National Assembly
12.45pm	Lunch
2.30pm	Meeting with CJ Entertainment & Creative Center for Convergence Culture
6.00pm	Presentation, Discussion and Dinner at Kim & Chang

Tuesday, January 17

9.30am	Guided Tour of Demilitarization Zone, UNCMAC, JSA Security Battalion, Tunnel 3, and Op Dora
3.00pm	Guided Tour of Samsung Innovation Center
4.30pm	Meeting with D. Camp

Wednesday, January 18

3.35pm	Travel to Tokyo, Japan

Thursday, January 19

09.30am	Departure from hotel
10.30am	Meeting with Smart News. Media App
1.00pm	Guided Tour of Meiji Shrine
3.30pm	Presentation and Dialogue with Nikkei Group

Friday, January 20

9.30am	Meeting at Riken
5.30pm	Dialogue on Fukushima Nuclear Accident by Kenji Tateiwa, Manager of Nuclear Power Programs

Saturday, January 21

Travel back to Boston

Asia Leadership Trek IX (Summer 2017)

Sunday, May 28

	Travel to Manila

Monday, May 29

9.30am	Guided Tour at Lopez Museum and Library
1.00pm	Meeting with Asian Development Bank, Country Specialist, Suchin Teoh
4.00pm	Meeting with Enderun College, Dr. Edgardo Rodriguez
7.00pm	Dinner with Harvard Club of the Philippines

Tuesday, May 30

10.00am	Meeting with Partner of McKinsey Philippines, Anders Baerlund
1.00pm	Meeting with US Ambassador to Philippines, Sung Kim
4.00pm	Meeting and Networking Dinner with Speaker of Philippine Congress, Pantaleon Alvarez

Wednesday, May 31

9.00am	Meeting with Bloomberg Philippines, Anchor Tony Abad
11.00am	Meeting with President of Stratbase ADRi, Victor Manhit, and Former Foreign Affairs Secretary Albert Del Rosario
4.20pm	Travel to Hong Kong

Thursday, June 1

11.00am	Meeting with, Executive Director of Lan Kwai Fong Group, Fergus Fung
2.00pm	Meeting at Red Cross Hong Kong

Appendix I | Trek and Fellowship Itinerary 235

Friday, June 2

9.00am	Meeting with Vice President of Hong Kong University of Science and Technology, Dr. Eden Woon
4.15pm	Meeting with CEO of Hong Kong Science & Technology Park, Albert Wong

Saturday, June 3

Free Time

Sunday, June 4

Travel to Shanghai

Monday, June 5

9.30am	Meeting with CEO and Partner of Anomaly Shanghai, Eric Lee
12.00pm	Meeting and lunch with David Harmon of Huawei
2.30pm	Meeting with CFO and Vice President of NIKE Greater China, Gavin Lindberg

Tuesday, June 6

9.00am	Guided Tour of Alibaba Global Leadership Academy
	Asia Leadership Seminar at Alibaba
11:50am - 12:05pm	"Teaching Intelligent People How to Learn", TED-style Talk by Peter Deutscher, Harvard Kennedy School
12:05pm - 13:15pm	Three (3) Workshops by ALT (Possible Topics are: "Design Thinking" by Jennifer Hurford, Harvard Business School; "Adapting to Change," by Peter Deutscher, HKS; "Building High Impact Teams" by Emily Gannam, Fletcher School of Law and Diplomacy
13:15pm - 13:30pm	Closing Remarks and Networking and Refreshments
	Conference at Zhejiang High School

2:15pm - 2:30pm	Center for Asia Leadership Introduction
2:30pm - 3:20pm	Forum Talk Show
3:30pm - 4:20pm	Entrepreneurship 101, Benedikt Groever, Networking 101, Catherine Keane, Applying to U.S. Universities: Writing a Statement of Purpose, Takuya Takeda; Bringing Your Story Alive: Connecting Your What to Your Why, Emily Gannam, Negotiation Tools for Everyday Situations, Soichiro Suzuki, Tips for Picking the Right Career, Jennifer Hurford

Wednesday, June 7

9.00am	Meeting at Wall Street Journal, James T. Areddy
1.00pm	Meeting with Principal of Shanghai Studios, Benjamin T. Wood
3.00pm	Guided Tour at K11 Art Mall and Dahvida Falanitule

Thursday, June 8

1.35am	Travel to Kuala Lumpur
9.00am	Meeting with CEO of Takaful Malaysia, YBhg. Dato' Seri Mohamed Hassan Bin Md. Kamil
1.15pm	Meeting with Trustee of Yayasan Chow Kit, Tunku Zain Abidin and Founder, Dr Hartini Zainudin
4.00pm	Meeting with Executive Editor-in-Chief of Sin Chew Media Group, Kuik Cheng Kang

Friday, June 9

11.00am	Meeting with CEO of Citibank, Lee Lung Nien
4.00pm	Meet and Greet with Teaching Assistants

Appendix I | Trek and Fellowship Itinerary 237

Saturday, June 10

9.00am - 6.00pm	**Asia Leadership Conference 2017 in Sunway University**
9.00am	Welcome Remarks by Co-Founder and President of Center for Asia Leadership Hungsoo S. Kim, TED- style Talk "Learning How to Learn" by Peter Deutscher Plenary by Co-Founder and President of Center for Asia Leadership Hungsoo S. Kim, Workshop A Professional Development
12.50pm	Lunch / Prayers
2.00pm	Workshop B Career Mentoring
4.40pm	Panel Discussion "New Perspective on Leadership" by Moderator. Emily Gannam; Panelists. Jennifer Hurford, Puay Siang Tan, Raza Ahmad Closing Remarks by Senior Executive Director of Sunway Education Group & Sunway University, Dr Elizabeth Lee
5.00pm	End

Sunday, June 11

8.00am	Free Time
3.00pm	Travel to Singapore

Monday, June 12

2.00pm	Meeting at Singapore Airlines
8.00pm	Observation and Meeting of Political Process in Local Singapore Community

Tuesday, June 13

11.00am	Meeting at iExperience (IMDA Singapore)
3.00pm	Meeting with Head of Asia Insights and Head of Strategy and Transformation of DBS

| 5:30pm | Meeting with People's Action Party Representatives, Minister of State Janil Puthucheary, Discussion on Singapore's smart nation initiatives |

Wednesday, June 14

| 10.00am | Meeting with Ambassador Bilahari Kausikan |
| 7.10pm | Travel to Dhaka |

Thursday, June 15

10.00am	Dialogue with head of UNDP Access to Information (a2i) Project of the Prime Minister's Office, Anir Chowdhury
11.45am	Director of LICT Project Md. Rezaul Karim & Component Team Leader Sami Ahmed, Information and Communication Technology Division and LICT Project
12.30pm	Meeting with Senior Facilitator of Standard Chartered Bangladesh Learning Academy, Tyseer Amin
2.00pm	Dialogue with MicroEnsure Representatives
3.30pm	Meeting with US Embassy, Public Affairs, Secretary Rex Moser
6.00pm	Meeting with CEO Axiata Limited Robi Nowshad

Friday, June 16

9.00am	Meeting with Radio Next Presenter, Nahiyan Naser
11.00am	Meeting with Expo Freight Limited Representatives
1.00pm	Meeting with Jamuna Future Park/Jamuna TV

Saturday, June 17

6.30am	Guided Tour at Garments Factory Dialogue with Ananta Group Bangladesh Representatives
12.00pm	Meeting with Director of University of Dhaka Institute of Business Administration Dr. Saiful Majid
2.00pm	Dialogue with Country Director of Save the Children, Mark Pierce

| Appendix II |
List of Trekkers and Fellows

• • •

Asia Leadership Trek 2017

Can (Jeff) Cui, *American*
MBA, Harvard Business School

Catherine Yuen Wah Lee, *Canadian*
MBA, Harvard Business School

Daiki Tajima, *Japanese*
MALD, Tufts Fletcher School of Law and Diplomacy

Dang Nguyen, *American*
Research Fellow in Medicine, Harvard Medical School

Professor Gil Alterovitz, *American*
Director of Biomedical Cybernetics Laboratory, Harvard Medical School

Giacomo Giorgio Canepa Declercq, *Peruvian*
MALD, Tufts Fletcher School of Law and Diplomacy

Jia Wen Hoe, *Singaporean*
MPP, Harvard Kennedy School of Government

Jasdeep Randhawa, *Indian*
MPP, Harvard Kennedy School of Government

John Lim, *Canadian/Filipino*
Yonsei/Fletcher, Harvard Extension School

Justin Hartley, *Australian*
MPA, Harvard Kennedy School of Government

Kyunga (Chloe) Jeong, *Korean*
BSc. Management, State University of New York, Binghamton

Louis Miguel Cotti, *American*
MALD, Tufts Fletcher School of Law and Diplomacy

Mizuki Nakamura, *Japanese*
Bachelor of Law, Keio University

Orianne Montaubin, *French/Thai*
MBA, Harvard Business School

Phillip Isaac Shattan, *American*
MALD, Tufts Fletcher School of Law and Diplomacy

Rahul Srinivasan, *Indian*
MPA, Harvard Kennedy School, MPA

Ralph Poettinger, *Austrian*
National University of Singapore
LLM, East China University of Political Science and Law

Samuel Hungsoo Kim, *Korean*
MPA, Harvard Kennedy School /
Kellogg School of Management

Seokjoon Moon, *Korean*
MPP, Harvard Kennedy School of Government

Ulrich Kopetzki, *Austrian*
Visiting Scholar, Northwestern Kellogg School of Management

Wilson Kyi, *American*
MBA, Harvard Business School

Yoshiko Takase, *Japanese*
MALD, Tufts Fletcher School of Law and Diplomacy

Zhaoying Xu, *Chinese*
PhD, Harvard University / Harvard Medical School

●●●

Asia Leadership Trek IX (Summer 2017)

Ahmad Raza, *American*
MALD, Tufts Fletcher School of Law and Diplomacy

Benedikt Groever, *German*
PhD, Harvard School of Engineering and Applied Sciences

Catherine Keane, *American*
Ed.M, Harvard Graduate School of Education

Emily Gannam, *American*
MALD, Tufts Fletcher School of Law and Diplomacy

Jennifer Hurford, *American*
MBA & MPP, Harvard Business School & Harvard Kennedy School

John Lim, *Canadian/Filipino*
Yonsei/Fletcher, Harvard Extension School

Orianne Montaubin, *French/Thai*
MBA, Harvard Business School

Peter Deutscher, *Australian*
MPP, Harvard Kennedy School

Samuel Hungsoo Kim, *Korean*
MPA, Harvard Kennedy School /
Kellogg School of Management

Sheikh Mohammed Irfan, *Bangladesh*
National University of Singapore

Suzuki Soichiro, *Japanese*
MALD, Tufts Fletcher School of Law and Diplomacy

Takuya Takeda, *Japanese*
MALD, Tufts Fletcher School of Law and Diplomacy

Puay Siang Tan, *Singaporean*
Masters in System Design and Management, Massachusetts Institute of Technology (MIT)

Yutaro Hokari, *Japanese*
MALD, Tufts Fletcher School of Law and Diplomacy

● ● ●

Asia Leadership Fellowship 2017

Ahmad Raza, *American*
MALD, Tufts Fletcher School of Law and Diplomacy

Ami Jean Valdemoro, *American/Filipino*
MPP, Harvard Kennedy School

Craig Brimhall, *American*
Ed. M, Harvard Graduate School of Education

Helen van Baal, *German*
M. Sc., Imperial College London

John Lim, *Canadian/Filipino*
Yonsei/Fletcher, Harvard Extension School

Dr. Namit Choksi, *Indian*
MPH, Harvard School of Public Health

Orianne Montaubin, *French/Thai*
MBA, Harvard Business School

Panche Kralev, *American*
MPP, Harvard Kennedy School

Samuel Hungsoo Kim, *Korean*
MPA, Harvard Kennedy School /
Kellogg School of Management

www.ingramcontent.com/pod-product-compliance
Lightning Source LLC
Chambersburg PA
CBHW052145220526
45471CB00004B/1539